He Captured My Heart!

My Story of Love

Waveney V. Martinborough

TEACH Services, Inc.
P U B L I S H I N G
www.TEACHServices.com • (800) 367-1844

World rights reserved. This book or any portion thereof may not be copied or reproduced in any form or manner whatever, except as provided by law, without the written permission of the publisher, except by a reviewer who may quote brief passages in a review.

The author assumes full responsibility for the accuracy of all facts and quotations as cited in this book. The opinions expressed in this book are the author's personal views and interpretations, and do not necessarily reflect those of the publisher.

This book is provided with the understanding that the publisher is not engaged in giving spiritual, legal, medical, or other professional advice. If authoritative advice is needed, the reader should seek the counsel of a competent professional.

Copyright © 2015 Waveney V. Martinborough

Copyright © 2015 TEACH Services, Inc.

ISBN-13: 978-1-4796-0570-5 (Paperback)

ISBN-13: 978-1-4796-0571-2 (ePub)

ISBN-13: 978-1-4796-0572-9 (Mobi)

Library of Congress Control Number: 2015914122

All Scripture, unless otherwise indicated, is taken from the New King James Version®. Copyright © 1982 by Thomas Nelson, Inc. Used by permission. All rights reserved.

Texted credited to KJV are taken from the King James Version Bible. Public domain.

Texts credited to Clear Word are from *The Clear Word,* copyright © 1994, 2000, 2003, 2004 by Review and Herald Publishing Association. All rights reserved.

Published by

www.TEACHServices.com • (800) 367-1844

Dedication

This book is dedicated to my precious children:
Esther Ann and husband, Marco; Samuel Neil; and John Erwin.

Gratitude

I am thankful to my eight siblings for the impact each of them has made on my life. And I am very grateful to my three dear children for their love and for the precious memories we have shared over the years. Special thanks goes to my dear husband, Gordon, my companion of fifty-two years, for helping to put some of the pieces of this story into place and for editing the manuscript. Above all, I am thankful to God for His miraculous guidance in my life, which is the theme of this book, and for His bringing back to my memory the various incidents of my love story.

Table of Contents

Introduction...9

Part One: Early Years..11
   Chapter 1 "Dear Land of Guyana"...............................13
   Chapter 2 Home, Sweet Home!...................................16
   Chapter 3 Childhood Experiences...............................20
   Chapter 4 Lessons Learned From My Siblings....................24
   Chapter 5 The Journey to Adventism............................29
   Chapter 6 Tappings on My Shoulder..............................34
   Chapter 7 In Hot Pursuit!...40

Part Two: Love, Marriage, and Ministry..................................46
   Chapter 8 Intersecting Pathways................................48
   Chapter 9 Love Is in the Air!....................................51
   Chapter 10 Here Comes the Bride!................................57
   Chapter 11 Our First District....................................62
   Chapter 12 Why, Lord? Why?......................................66
   Chapter 13 He Really Loves Me!..................................71

Part Three: First Stay in the United States...............................77
   Chapter 14 Arrival in America...................................79
   Chapter 15 Nursing Care Stories.................................83
   Chapter 16 Little Miracles......................................87
   Chapter 17 Ministry in San Diego................................92
   Chapter 18 Back at Loma Linda! Providence at Work!..............96
   Chapter 19 "Not Our Will, But Yours Be Done!"...................99

Part Four: Guyana, Caribbean, and Beyond.................................103
   Chapter 20 Climbing the Hill of Change..........................105
   Chapter 21 Shepherdess in Georgetown 1 District.................108
   Chapter 22 Back to the Workplace................................112

Chapter 23 Multiplied Miracles in Guyana Conference............117
Chapter 24 More Drama in Guyana............................122
Chapter 25 In the Land of the Hummingbird..................125

Part Five: Ministry at the Inter-American Division...........**131**
Chapter 26 Organizing a Brand New Department...............133
Chapter 27 "Happy in the Service of the King!".............138
Chapter 28 Educator and Evangelist.........................144
Chapter 29 Ups and Downs...................................152
Chapter 30 A New Day Dawns!................................159

Part Six: Happy Family Bible Seminars International..........**167**
Chapter 31 HFBSI Is Born!..................................169
Chapter 32 Miraculous Growth...............................174
Chapter 33 Success Stories.................................178
Chapter 34 "Plus Ultra!" There's More Beyond!..............180
Chapter 35 The Love of My Life!............................182

Bibliography **188**

Introduction

I was overjoyed that day I met Him. I felt like jumping to the ceiling. No, I did not meet Him on eHarmony, neither on the popular reality show "The Bachelor," nor on any social media. I was all alone that day when I heard Him say, "I love you! I have always loved you!" That memorable day He captured my heart and continues to hold it very close.

In this book, I am sharing with you my exciting love story. It is a love story with a difference. It is my story. Everyone has a story. While it is true that many biographies are written to exalt one's self, that is not my intent. Yes, it has some "horn tooting," but as my friend Milton used to say, "if thou tootest not thine own horn, by whomever will it be tooted?" However it endeavors to demonstrate the love of God, and the exploits He can help us accomplish if we submit to His leadership. Like the stories in the Bible, I have included—as far as my memory permitted—details of my life that are both good and not so good.

And this story is written as a legacy not only to my three children, but also to the children of relatives and friends, to children of my extended family in the church and school, as well as to all God's children everywhere. It is to encourage each one to take Jesus as their Lover and Friend. As you read, may you be inspired.

Part One:

Early Years

Chapter 1

"Dear Land of Guyana"

The Best of Times

It was on a bright September morning that I was born in the village of Beterverwagting in the country of Guyana. I would never know if my mother said, "Not another girl!" You see, she unashamedly said that she loved boys, and I was girl number five! God blessed her with nine children—seven girls and two boys.

Guyana, which was formerly British Guiana, is the only English-speaking country in South America, and is bordered by Surinam or Dutch Guiana, Brazil, Venezuela, and the Atlantic Ocean. It has three great rivers—Essequibo, Demerara, and Berbice—that divide the country into three distinct counties. There are six races—the native Amerindians (like the American Indians), Africans who came as slaves, East Indians who came as indentured workers, Europeans, Chinese, and Portuguese. In addition, there are many people of mixed races.

At the time of my birth, the three quarter million people lived mostly on the coastline of the country. But the wealth of the land lay in the hinterland where timber, gold, and diamonds could be found. The other staples were bauxite, rice, sugar, and the famous intoxicating demerara rum. However, its greatest wealth was its happy good-natured people, who achieved a high level of education.

In the best of times, Guyana was a beautiful country. People were attracted to the well laid out, clean, and strategically located city of Georgetown, which was proudly called the

Garden City. The Atlantic Ocean on the north provided the northeast trade winds to cool the heat during the blistering summer months. And for the tourist there was the mighty Kaieteur Falls with its perpendicular drop of 721 feet that was accessible by air or the long treacherous mountain climb.

The Worst of Times!

In the 1950s several young, brilliant nationals like Cheddie Jagan (with his wife Janet, a Russian communist), Linden Forbes Samson Burnham, Sydney King, Hamilton Green, and others formed the powerful People's Progressive Party. Under the leadership of Dr. Jagan, the PPP won a landslide victory in 1957. The Burhman faction soon split from the PPP and formed the PNC (People's National Congress). This caused a split in the country along racial lines—East Indians aligned with Jagan and blacks with Burnham; violence followed. There were lootings, killings, and burnings in the city and country alike. The cry of "race for race" caused blacks to move out of Indian areas and vice versa. And the Chinese, whose stores were looted, fled to the safety of other countries.

After the 1964 elections, the PNC formed a coalition with the United Force, and Burnham became Prime Minister. Under his leadership the country gained independence from Britain, the "colonial masters" as they were called. On May 26, 1966, after a week of celebration, we lifted our voices and sang for the last time, "God save our gracious Queen," as the Union Jack was lowered. Then ear-splitting cheers rent the starry sky as they hoisted the Golden Arrow—the red, green, black, and white flag of Guyana. As the conductor lifted his baton, the police band struck the note and the people joined in singing for the very first time our own national anthem:

Green land of Guyana of rivers and plains

Made rich by the sunshine and lush by the rain

Set gemlike and fair between mountains and sea

Our children salute you Dear land of the free.

However, sad to say, the high expectations of a prosperous Guyana under brilliant national leaders were soon dashed to pieces! The economy of this socialist state deteriorated. Basic food items like milk, cheese, flour, peas, and beans became scarce. Long periods of "black outs" because of low electrical power was an everyday affair. There was control of travel and currency. The last group of expatriates left when the bauxite and sugar companies were nationalized. Many who wanted Burnham in now wished him out. And he did not seem to care. He had the power but lacked the support. It was indeed "the worst of times" for our dear land of Guyana.

Added to the dismay of all was the Jim Jones saga that put Guyana on the map and its name on the lips of much of the world. With the promise of a better life, this American-born cult leader seduced many US citizens, took them to the hinterland of Guyana, robbed them of their freedom, rights, privileges, and possessions, made them cut the towering trees to build a compound, and kept them well guarded and obedient only to him. All this was unknown to the Guyanese public until the news of a mass suicide in the interior. Their tragic end came unexpectedly after the US government intervened and their leader gave his followers the cyanide-based potion to drink. More than five hundred Americans lost their lives. What a tragedy!

Beterverwagting

The place of my childhood was the village called Beterverwagting, abbreviated BV. It is derived from the Dutch words "Beter verwachting." Leaving the public highway that connected the counties of Demerara and Berbice, and entering the village, the second house was our home. It was about a five minute walk from the Atlantic Ocean, and was identifiable by the word Magnel scripted in bold Old English letters.

Since the coastland was below sea level, a sea wall was built to keep back the ocean surge and prevent flooding at high tide. On evenings we could hear the waves as they dashed themselves against the wall. Houses were built high on stilts, trenches lined the road that led into the village to prevent flooding when the dyke was opened, and bridges were built across the trenches to access each home. Opposite our house was a large playing field or park for cricket, picnics, or village activities.

We lived comfortably in our three-bedroom home with the usual living room, dining area, a common area we called the pantry, a large kitchen, and a yard with all kinds of tropical fruit trees such as julie mango, gunep, downes, jamun, pomegranate, guava, guanabana or sour sop, a citrus hybrid called shaddock, coconut trees, and a large breadfruit tree. Overhanging the bridge was a weeping willow or pine tree that provided the Christmas tree for many city folk, but made the bridge hazardous in the rainy season.

Two tanks provided us with rain water, and one of us had the chore of transporting the water from the tank downstairs to a covered drum in the kitchen to provide water for cooking and washing dishes, and to a clay goblet where we kept water for drinking. Water from the goblet was a cool refreshing drink as if it came from a refrigerator. That refreshing water was a fitting symbol of the joy and peace I felt in our country home nestled in our "Dear land of Guyana!"

Beterverwagting means "better expectation." That's what God had for me, and that's what He has for you – regardless of where you were born.

Beterverwagting means "better expectation." That's what God had for me, and that's what He has for you – regardless of where you were born. It is comforting to know that He remembers where each of us was born! The psalmist says, "The Lord will record, when He registers the peoples: 'This one was born there'" (Ps. 87:6).

Chapter 2

Home, Sweet Home!

The Breadwinner

My dad's name was Harold Eric Hinds, lovingly referred to as "H.E." Dad worked as an accountant at Enmore Estates about eight miles from BV and seventeen miles from Georgetown. Because of transportation difficulties, he stayed at Enmore much of the week and returned home on Saturday afternoons. We would look for him and run to meet him and help him with the gallon-sized can of rich cow's milk from which Mom made rich homemade butter. Sometimes he would also have goodies such as a delicious Swiss roll.

What was amazing to us children was how quickly Dad could add the columns of figures and give the right answer without the use of an adding machine. Dad was definitely not a talker; he was a worker! And he worked diligently to provide for his family. What I admired about him was that he did not smoke, and he seldom drank. I used to watch what he did when his friends came by. He would light up and have the cigarette by his side until it smoked itself out! And when they poured the liquor into the wine glass, he would just take a sip or two. It made me decide that I would marry someone who, like my dad, would neither smoke nor drink. Parents teach by both precept and example, and as we all know, what we do is more effective than what we say. So parents, watch your example!

Dad was a churchgoer. On most Sunday mornings we would gather for family worship and then he would go to the Anglican or

Chapter 2 Home, Sweet Home!

Episcopalian Church where he participated in the service. I was especially impressed with the Good Friday service. The women dressed in white to commemorate the death of Jesus on the cross. And even as children, we had to honor the day. We cleaned the house, could not play, and got no lunch until after the three-hour watch from noon to 3:00 p.m. to commemorate the death of Christ on the cross.

The Homemaker

Mom told us that her dream was to be a businesswoman. And she would have been a shrewd successful one! Instead she became a schoolteacher. However, after marriage she did not continue with her profession. In those days a woman's place was definitely in the home. So she became a homemaker, and our mother loved us and she disciplined us.

Here is an incident that I believe Aubrey, my younger brother, always remembered. Mom told us that when eating genup we should bite and crush its seed to avoid choking. One day my little brother tried eating this fruit, and the seed slipped down his throat, blocking his airways. With hands flaying in the air, he gasped for breath. While my eldest sister, Cynthia, not knowing the Heimlich maneuver, tried to take it out with her finger, my bigger brother, Rudolph, shouted, "Hit the boy's back!" She hit his back so hard that the seed flew out of his mouth! Mom then got up from her sewing machine, and without saying a word, gave him a reminder with the rod, which, as Solomon said, would drive his disobedience "far from him."

But Mom's discipline was equally matched by her love, which she lavished upon all her children. While there were not the spoken words "I love you" nor the physical hugs and kisses, she showed her love by her actions. She never shouted at us, and she took care of all our needs. She made sure we went to school on time with a good breakfast of cereal, milk, and bread with either butter or cheese, jam or avocado. Lunch was ready when we returned home at noon, and dinner was prepared by 5:00 p.m. She was always at home to greet us at the end of the day, and whenever she had to be away unexpectedly, she always left a note to tell where she was and what we should do. She ensured that we had food supplements like cod liver oil, Scotch emulsion, and our favorite malt. Of course, we knew that she preferred the boys to the girls, but she never showed favoritism to any child. She loved us all the same.

Mom was also a "medicine woman!" During the year we were given bitters, to "bitter the blood," and in the last week of the long summer vacation she used a cleansing concoction. For three days she administered her potions. First was chamomile, which she claimed was to "gather the bile." Next came the mixture of Epson salts and boiled senna leaves (the senna that is now commercialized as a herbal tea). Then, if necessary, on the third day was the dreaded castor oil. These potions not only tasted badly, they also caused stomach cramps. In addition, we were given warm barley tea and told to drink lots of water. However, at the end of this ordeal, she prepared a sumptuous meal to satisfy our hungry "cleansed" stomachs.

One thing was certain, we always had lots to eat! For breakfast there was hot cereal with milk, homemade bread with cheese, homemade guava jam, or avocado. For lunch and dinner, the staple was rice served with vegetables, and either beans, fish, shrimp, or beef. One specialty was "cooked up rice," which was rice cooked with coconut milk and either split peas, black eye peas, or pigeon peas. Another was called *metagee*, which was ground provisions cooked in coconut milk. The Sunday special was soup with much meat, ground provisions, and *fofo*, boiled plantains pounded in a wooden mortar and formed into a ball.

The Christmas morning special was pepper-pot—a Guyanese delicacy of beef cooked in a spiced Amerindian sauce called *casareep*. At this festive season, we also had apples imported from the United States, homemade ice cream churned the old fashioned way, homemade cookies, beef patties, pine tarts, and other special treats. Then there was the five-pound black liquored fruit cake she baked and served to family and friends.

All through the year we enjoyed a variety of local fruit—mango, banana, star apple, guava, and papaya, which we reaped from our home garden or the farm. Some days we had so many mangoes that we skipped a cooked meal and ate as many mangoes as we wanted! We did the same when sweet potatoes were harvested. No wonder we needed the "cleansing!"

Mom's generosity extended far and wide. Each day she sent lunch to an elderly single shut-in lady, and on Sundays she shared her split pea soup to some of the sick she knew in the community, which we had to carry before we ate! No beggar who came through her gate was ever turned away empty. Nor was she afraid to entertain strangers. I remember once a Portuguese man with uncontrollable shakes and impaired speech who came asking for food to eat and a place to stay. Mom fed him and made a bed for him in the kitchen. The next morning when we awoke he was already gone. One Saturday afternoon a woman from the city came asking to stay for the night. She ended up staying for two weeks, enjoying our hospitality but helping to do nothing! Eventually mom had to ask her to leave.

The Supporter

As children, we attended the Congregational Church with our dear Grandma Betsy, lovingly called "Ba." We loved her because she would help us with our chores, give us a penny or two from her pension, take us out on Saturday nights to visit her sister, and buy crushed ice cones with syrup on the way back home. She was the one who took time to braid our hair after Mom had washed it. It took so long to gently comb out the kinks that most times we went to sleep with our head in her lap. She told us stories. I remember her telling us the story of the Titanic, how quickly the merry-making turned to despair when the massive "unsinkable" ship began to sink, and how the passengers started singing, "Nearer my God to Thee, Nearer to Thee!"

She also helped Mom with ironing our clothes using the flat iron that was heated on burning coals in what we called a coal pot. Well, one morning she was ironing and somehow two- or three-year-old little Aubrey got his foot caught between the bed and the wall. Grandma, forgetting that she had the hot iron in her hand, ran to his rescue. Somehow Mom could not understand why the poor child was screaming at the top of his lungs until she looked and saw that the hot iron in Grandma's hand was pressing against his body! Thank God he was not badly burnt. I think he still has the scar to this day.

When I was in secondary school, preparing to take the Higher Senior Oxford examination, Ba suffered a stroke that affected her mentally, and she began behaving in strange ways to the point of attacking anyone in her way with her raised fist. She became so fierce that once we had to lock her in her room, and when there she ripped open the mattress on her bed and threw all of its contents through her bedroom window. Lyn, her favorite grandchild, was the only one able to control her.

One of the last things she did was to plant a plantain stalk in the garden. It produced a huge

Chapter 2 Home, Sweet Home!

bunch of plantains that served us for days. Like so many others, she planted but did not reap. I am so glad that the prophet Isaiah assures us that in the new earth we will eat what we plant (Isa. 65:22). I must tell you that one day, before she took her bed for the last time, she ate almost all of curried chicken that the family was to eat for dinner with the *rhoti* that our Indian neighbor had prepared for us. It was a lot of chicken—enough for nine of us! Within a week or so, she passed to her rest.

I saw her die that memorable Sunday morning. Her sister Aunt Minnie and my sisters Magnel and Lynette were giving her a bed bath. She was lying on her stomach as they washed her back, and when they turned her over, her chest rose up and down as she struggled for oxygen. Seconds later she took her final breath. She was laid to rest that very afternoon. My tears flowed as I saw the casket being loaded in the hearse that took her to her final resting place. I look forward to seeing her in our heavenly home where we will not sing her favorite song, "Someone will enter the pearly gates," but "the song of Moses and the Lamb." She had a beautiful voice, and I'm planning to blend my voice with hers, and yours! That will be the ultimate "Home, Sweet Home!"

Chapter 3

Childhood Experiences

I enjoyed a typical childhood. I ran, hopped, skipped, played with broomstick dolls, played "teacher" to the pillars of the house, and enjoyed making mud pies. And they were so "delicious" as my siblings and I pretended to eat them while we chatted at our "tea party." Since we had few friends, we played all kinds of games among ourselves. These included board checkers, marble checkers, monopoly, and even chess. The favorite outdoor game was cricket.

Fascinating!

In the evenings we listened as our elders told us true to life stories, jokes, and scary ghost stories. My grandmother told us about "Ole Higue." According to her, the Ole Higues were mostly women who could get out of their skin, turn into balls of fire, and get into homes to suck the blood of helpless babies who sometimes died. She often told us that she would see them in the night in the cemetery not far from her window—we lived near two cemeteries. But although we asked her to awaken us to see them, she never did! We later conjectured that what she saw were lightning bugs or fireflies, which we called "candle flies."

Almost every active child experiences injury. I had my share of them. One evening I was tossed by our cow Blackie when my big brother put me on its back as Mom was milking it. Another time I was bitten by one of Ba's sheep. I had allowed it to lick the molasses off my hand, and when the sweet substance was

Chapter 3 Childhood Experiences

finished, the sheep bit down on my fingers and would not let go! I had to box its ears to get rid of it. My most terrifying experience, however, was when I stepped on an upturned rusty nail. Even now I cringe as I remember how Mom pulled it out and treated it every day using primitive methods that would make modern medicine blush. And while playing a game of cricket, my sister Maisie hit a ball that connected with my left eye. It has affected that eye to this day, making it difficult to read the letters in ophthalmologist's office. I now have a cataract in that eye that needs to be removed.

My most terrifying experience, however, was when I stepped on an upturned rusty nail... Mom pulled it out and treated it every day using primitive methods that would make modern medicine blush.

I was often plagued by malaria, which is carried by the female Anopheles mosquito. With this strange illness, I would be very sick with fever in the morning but feel well in the afternoon. Every time the pharmacist, known to all as Dr. P, dispensed the effective quinine tablets, he would sing his usual tune, "Drink barley water, soda water, no biscuits." (My son-in-law Marco and his team are working to discover in their lab a one-time injection to cure this dreadful disease. May their dream soon become a reality.)

Learning

In school, teachers used the rod freely. This was done not only to curb bad behavior, but also to motivate children to learn. I was basically a good student and was usually the last child that the teacher would call on to answer a question. So I rarely had to succumb to the pain of the teacher's strong right arm. However, one day I volunteered to go to the chalkboard to show the class how to solve a math problem. With confidence I started writing "1 pencil cost..." *Whack! Whack!* That was the sound of the teacher's whip on my back as she shouted, "1 pencil costs!" So I added the "s" to cost.

Then I continued, "78 pencils costs ..." *Whack! Whack!* Again I felt the sting of another lash on my back as she bellowed "cost!" This eight year old was confused until she said, "1 pencil **costs**, more than one **cost!**" That day I went home with my back sore. Mom put some heat on it and promised to go to the teacher, but she never did. In the midst of a math lesson, I had learned a lesson in English grammar! As I recall, after that incident she was absent for a long while. We later learned that she had passed away. She used to have regular nosebleeds.

Maxims or proverbial sayings in bold letters dotted the walls of the school. Some I remember are "Knowledge is power!" "If you fail to prepare, you prepare to fail." We also learned poems like this one: "Figure it out for yourself my lad / You've all that the greatest of men have had / Two arms, two hands, two legs, two eyes / And a brain to use if you would be wise / With this equipment they all began / So start for the top and say 'I Can!'" (author unknown). And the apostle Paul quickly reminds us, "I can do all things through Christ who strengthens me" (Phil. 4:13).

Can you imagine seeing me in a fight? Well, I was in a fight with a classmate. We both attended the BV Government School. I don't recall the trigger, but I was urged on by some of my friends who chanted, "Fire, fire, bun my hand!" I was the first to accept the challenge and gave the first blow. But she was taller, and after she returned my punch, I swallowed my pride and called it quits. I quickly learned my lesson and determined never to fight again.

Dangerous!

My sister Maisie and I did a lot of things together. One dangerous thing we did was to bend down and pass under the freight train so that we could get to school in time to play. In those days the trains had steam engines, and these needed to refill their water supply. The BV station had a water tank for this purpose. When trains stopped for water, they would block the roadway and pedestrians had to wait until the refilling was over. While we waited we saw others taking the risk of passing under the carriage, and we proceeded to do likewise. But when we reached the other side, we ran right into the arms of someone who knew Mom, and she did not hesitate to remind us of the danger of doing such a thing.

One summer day we tried to go boating to Grandma's farmland beyond the village. Too eager for this adventure, we pushed off from the land with such force that the round bottom boat swayed from side to side and the next thing we knew we were all in the water under an overturned boat! Thank God the water was not deep. We had to abort the trip and return home drenched from head to toe.

I liked to dance and did it gracefully. The norm for us on Saturday nights after sunset was to turn on the radio and practice the latest moves during the fifteen-minutes calypso music program. One evening the radio stopped working, and for months it lay dormant since Mom was in no hurry to fix it. That was the end of the Saturday night dance lessons! I had another opportunity to dance when Mom and I attended my aunt's wedding. I was dancing with a school friend when an older man bumped him and took his place. Mother Iris, who was always watching out for her children, saw it and calmly escorted me back to my seat! I did not ask her why—in those days children did not question parents—but as I grew older I learned that dancing raises intense sexual emotions that could lead to inappropriate behavior. I believe God winked at my innocence.

If you look carefully, you will see a dimple on my cheek. However, it's only on my right side, so it is not natural! How did it get there? I was returning home one afternoon when I saw workmen repairing the road, and right opposite our bridge was a giant stone crusher with its huge iron rollers looking like a monster! Fear gripped my heart and I started to run. But rain had fallen, and the bridge was slippery. Suddenly I slipped and fell, and the pointed edge of my broken slate punctured my jaw. And when it healed, there was a dimple!

Amazing!

We always had pets—cats and dogs. There was Blackie, a good watchdog; playful Tricksie; and Pom Pom who was by no means an aggressive dog but was noted for his select eating habits. One of our neighbors, whom we called "Uncle," raised cows and a fat mother pig that gave birth to about seven piglets. One day one of them found a space under the fence and crossed over into our yard. Our dog took one look at it and with one snap and a tiny squeak its life was over! Strange enough, the dog did not have this tongue-licking delicacy for its dinner; he simply walked away from the carcass. And would you believe it? That was the

Chapter 3 Childhood Experiences

fate of each of the piglets as one by one they crossed into Pom Pom's territory! Sad to say, every time Uncle saw that his source of income decreased or his pork chops vanished, he would come to the fence and say, "He's gone with another one!" We felt sorry for Uncle. Mom thought that it was simply amazing until she learned that our dog was complying with what God Himself told His people: The pig is an unclean creature, and should not be eaten (Lev. 11:7, 8).

I was a helpful child, willing to do whatever I was asked to do, but one Sunday I was not willing. My sister Magnel asked me to go to her friend and borrow her Latin text. We had two bicycles, and I thought that I could ride and return quickly. Instead I was told that I had to walk! And the hurtful thing is that I used to wash and polish those bikes as an act of love. I became very angry and left home grumbling to myself. When I was about a corner from the friend's house the tempter said, "Turn back now, and tell your sister that her friend was not at home." The other little voice said, "You might as well go on for the house is right there." To which voice did I listen? I was too mad to listen to the voice of reason and do the right thing. Already I tasted the sweet nectar of revenge! So I returned home and told the lie. More than that, I kept very quiet when the next day my sister said that her friend told her that she was at home but no one came. Someone rightly said, "If you always want to get even with others, you'll never get ahead" (author unknown).

Don't play with fire! This is the lesson Maisie and I learned one afternoon when we were melting the polish used for polishing wooden floors. We thought nothing of the little fire until it flared up and was too big for us to put out. I was so scared that I could not say what was happening. It could have been disastrous had it not been for the agility and quick thinking of Grandma soaking the mat in water and using it to put out the flames. Today there are other fires with which we should not play! Some of them are drugs, sex, and social media.

As I write about my childhood memories, I think about Jesus as a child. In two short verses, the Bible summarizes those years of His life. "And the Child grew and became strong in spirit, filled with wisdom; and the grace of God was upon Him.… And Jesus increased in wisdom and stature, and in favor with God and man" (Luke 2:40, 52). But the jolting thought is that as a child the tempter was always at His heels trying to get Him to do naughty things as well. "Satan was unwearied in his efforts to overcome the Child of Nazareth.… He left no means untried to ensnare Jesus" (White, *The Desire of Ages*, p. 71). The sobering thought is that if He had yielded to the devil one time only it would have disqualified Him from being our Savior! And then what would we have done? This makes me want to join William Featherstone and respond to the Savior's love by saying,

> My Jesus I love thee, I know Thou art mine
>
> For thee all the follies of sin I resign
>
> My gracious Redeemer, my Savior art thou
>
> If ever I loved thee, my Jesus, 'tis now.
>
> ("My Jesus, I Love Thee," 1864)

Don't you want to say that too?

Chapter 4
Lessons Learned From My Siblings

If you have lived with siblings you know that sometimes they are at their best and sometimes at their worst. I was born into a large family. I believe my mom and dad accepted God's directive to "be fruitful and multiply" and believed that "children are a heritage from the Lord ... Happy is the man who has his quiver full of them" (Ps. 127:3, 5). Their quiver had seven girls and two boys. And I was the symbol of perfection—number seven!

So what was it like to live with so many siblings? Most of the time it was fun! We did many things together. We played games, planted and worked in a garden, and worshiped at home and at church, singing and praying together. And we laughed a lot! If anything funny was said or done, especially at church, we had a special eye signal that went around that said, "take note." Then we joked about it around the dinner table!

Yes, we had our name-calling, provocations, and fights. But we learned that although we were all different we could accept those differences and live together. We learned to give and take, to forgive, to love and be loved, to develop tolerance and appreciation for others, and to use communication skills. We took pride in the family name and decided that we would do nothing to dishonor that name. As I grew older and realized that my identity was in Christ and that I was created in His image, I also decided that I did not want to dishonor His name—"Hallowed be Your name" (Matt. 6:9).

Chapter 4 Lessons Learned From My Siblings

One day Mom asked me if I would have liked to be an only child. "Yes!" I quickly answered as I thought of getting all the toys, attention, and care of my parents. But then I would have missed the different lifelong lessons I learned from each sibling that helped to shape my life until this day. So here is what I learned from listening and observing my siblings.

Sensitivity

Cynthia, fondly called JB, was the first. She was the first to attend Caribbean Union College (CUC), now University of the Southern Caribbean. After graduating, she worked as a teacher and vice principal of Harmon High School in Tobago. She later served as dean of women for the college. Cynthia later moved to the United States, graduated from Atlantic Union College, became a registered dietician, and worked at the large Jewish Bethesda Hospital in New York. She could keep you entertained for hours with stories of the Jewish culture, which she learned from her interaction with Jewish patients. In later years she married Bill who passed on before her; JB is now deceased.

One of the first lessons I learned from observing Cynthia is that behavior, whether good or bad, has consequences and that punishment for bad behavior can be painful. As the eldest child, she experienced a lot of discipline from Dad. Evidently Mom had adopted the "wait till your father gets home" policy, and he would use the "rod of correction" in an effort to drive the foolishness far from her (Prov. 22:15). We felt sorry for her and ganged up against Dad, not knowing that he did it in love. Even now I can feel the pain of others when they relate their hurts.

It was JB who first inspired me to attend CUC. I saw her face light up when she showed pictures of the place and the people, especially the young theology students. I admired the way she dressed for church and special occasions. She always looked as proud as a peacock. Doubtless I learned to dress well from her.

Love of learning

The second eldest sibling was Rudolph, fondly called "Hindsie." He was born on the island of Dominica. Gordon remembers him arriving at the BV church, taking off his jacket with care, and hanging it at the back of the chair, sitting with perfect posture with his back straight like an arrow, with his shoes as shiny as a mirror. His goal was medicine. After obtaining his bachelor's degree in biology from Oakwood College, now Oakwood University, he was accepted at Brandeis University to pursue his goal, but circumstances beyond his control diverted him. He went into the field of education and was principal of a high school in New York. He later completed his doctoral program. Rudolph is the father of Bridget Jackson (husband, Deryk) and Raymond Hinds (wife, Nadene) and is the grandfather of Danielle, Britanie, Christopher, and John.

Hindsie was the family's philosopher, and he liked to express his ideas with emphasis. I thought he knew a lot, and I wanted to know more. He inspired me with a love for learning. The first big word I heard from him, which sent me to the dictionary, was "vicissitudes," the ups and downs. When he traveled to America to attend Oakwood College, I wanted to go there also, even though he told of the racial divide that he experienced. For the first time in his life he was told that he could not be served at a particular restaurant. Thanks to the freedom fighters like defiant Rosa Parks and Dr. Martin Luther King, the Civil Rights Movement fought for the rights of all people.

Leadership

Lynette, whose birth certificate says Linet, and whom we fondly call Lyn, was also born in Dominica. She is a graduate of CUC/USC and Andrews University. On her return to Guyana from CUC, she served as a teacher and principal of the Adventist high school, and she later worked as an English teacher in Michigan. She is married to Dr. Ken Riley, and is the mother of Renee (husband, Michael), and grandmother of Khalil and Dominique.

Lyn was the intellectual. She always lamented that she had no childhood play days because the primary school principal saw her potential and coached her in the "scholarship class" with the goal of her getting the coveted four-year scholarship to the prestigious Bishop's High School.

In addition to being my French and algebra teacher in high school, Lynette taught me how to be a leader. I admired her frankness and the confidence she exhibited as our youth leader at the BV church. She led our choir, which received the blue ribbon at the Guyana Mission Music Festival, and she guided us in a successful Youth for Christ evangelistic campaign that resulted in four baptisms. She also taught me to be frugal when, for the first time, I saw a bank book. She was saving up for college! Lyn was the first sibling to obtain a graduate degree, which placed within me the desire to do graduate work whenever that became possible.

Diplomacy

Magnel, fondly called Mags, wanted to be a nurse since childhood. Mom often told us that before she could say the word, when asked what she wanted to become she would say, "a nor." She pursued her goal by completing a nursing program in Guyana. She then moved to England and graduated as a nurse midwife. She worked there for some time, and upon her return to Guyana, her career blossomed, and she assumed the responsibility of matron at Davis Memorial Hospital.

While growing up she had a temper, and her big brother recalls how one morning she had him dodging in the corner from the things that she hurled at him when he teased her. He learned his lesson and never stirred up her anger again!

I admire her spirituality. In England she was an elder of her church and several times was called upon to preach. Even now she continues to engage in Bible study, and she daily petitions the throne for her family members, especially her nieces and nephews. All would agree that she is very kind and overly careful in what she does, especially in food preparation.

Magnel is the diplomat. She could get you to do something without making you angry. When she came to our new home in Orlando, she suggested that for safety I needed to cover the glass panel beside the front door. I heard her but did nothing. When she came again she related incidents that she had heard on the news. The third time she gave ideas as to what I could do. Although she was persistent, I couldn't get angry with her. By her next visit, it was done! Jesus Himself said that we need to "be wise as serpents and harmless as doves" (Matt. 10:16).

Frugality

If you are to ask, "Mirror, mirror on the wall who is the fairest of them all?" It would be Thelma, my fifth sister, the middle one, who was fondly called Tello. After completing high school, she was the first to ask Mom to teach her to cook, and she became the manager of the home, leaving Mom free to move to Enmore to be with Daddy during the week.

Chapter 4 Lessons Learned From My Siblings

She managed so well that Mom had to commend her for the way she judiciously handled the financial affairs of the home, clearing the debt at Chin's Grocery. George, who lived less than a dozen houses from our home, had his eyes on her and mentioned it to his mother who came to our house. Apparently she and Mom made some kind of agreement because after George migrated to England he asked for her hand in marriage. She joined him a few months after, and soon wedding bells rang out at the Chiswick Seventh-day Adventist Church. She was the first sibling to get married. When Magnel and Maisie went to England to pursue their dreams, her home became their residence.

As I heard my mom commend her for clearing the debt at the BV grocery, I realized that being debt free was a good thing. So I kept it in mind and have practiced it up to this day despite the credit card offers and credit line of thousands of dollars available. I also noted her courage when she decided to travel across the Atlantic by boat for fourteen days to marry George Cadogan whom she hardly knew but who was a close friend of her older brother. So was that love, stupidity, or faith? They recently celebrated fifty-five years of marriage! She is the mother of six, grandmother of nine, and great grandmother of two. And her children—Faye, Arnold, Andrew, Paul, Jeffrey, Peter—are extremely devoted to her since the recent death of her husband, their father. She has been a good wife and mother.

Adventurous Spirit

Maisie, fondly called Mais, was at one time called Mennen. While growing up, she and I did a lot of things together. She was full of adventure, and along with my younger brother, we did a lot of daring things together. One Sabbath afternoon we caught ten crabs at the swamp near the beach and crushed many Portuguese man-of-war and heard them pop without getting stung! She tends to be bossy and, just like me, can be stubborn! Maisie also pursued a nursing program in England and graduated as a nurse midwife. She worked in England, Guyana, and New York. Living in the Big Apple, she continued her studies and graduated as a nurse anesthetist. Mom always said she would have made a good medical doctor if she had had the opportunity. She has one daughter, Denise, and four grandchildren—Kaylan, Kaija, Kethan, and Keston.

Just like Mom, Mais is a good businesswoman, and her adventurous spirit enabled her to engage in profitable business transactions. She purchased properties in both New York and Orlando and has hosted her two unmarried sisters. This spirit of adventure became an asset to me, especially as I embarked on the unchartered territory of being the first women's ministries director of the sprawling Inter-American Division. I also admire Maisie's generosity. She is always ready to help others in time of need. As kids, she, Aubrey, and I were called the "three musketeers!"

Love of Music

Ruby, fondly called Rubes, is the last daughter. As children we did not spend much time together because she lived with Mother Lily, our next-door neighbor. In that four-bedroom house lived Uncle and Auntie, a childless couple who were the owners; Mother Lily and Aunt B, sisters of Uncle; and Teacher B and her brother, the niece and nephew of Auntie. As children we were always welcome there. Ruby was like their spoiled child who got whatever she wanted.

Ruby bravely worked as a missionary teacher among the Amerindians in the hinterland village of Paraima. Then she went on to CUC and graduated from the secretarial science program. For years she worked as an administrative secretary to the administrator of Port of Spain Adventist Community Hospital in Trinidad. She married Clyde Sallion and is the mother of Dr. Carolyn and Michelle and grandmother of five.

Aunt B taught Ruby to play the piano. Hearing her play made me want to play the piano also. After teaching myself, I can play some of the hymns, and I often "entertain" my husband in the morning as he encourages me by singing along. I also taught myself to play the accordion and mouth organ. When I lived in Trinidad, Ruby and I got close to each other, and we would connect by phone several times a week, while her husband Clyde, who was a very good mechanic, took care of our cars at a moment's notice. She also taught me that in order to have friends, one should be friendly. Not only was she a friend to me when we were the only siblings in Trinidad, but she was a friend to many church members who became a valuable support system after her husband's sudden demise.

Spiritual Focus

Aubrey, whose fond name is Stannie, is the last of the Hinds clan. As a child he loved to attend every funeral in the village regardless of the person's race or religion. However, one day this came to a screeching halt when he saw the corpse of Miss X and her daughter, whose brutal murder rocked the peace and quiet of our little village. Her intended son-in-law axed her and his intended bride, set the house on fire, then turned the gun on himself. After Stannie saw those hacked bodies, his funeral days were over!

Aubrey graduated from Columbia Union College, then worked as a laboratory technician, and later as supervisor of Washington Adventist Hospital, Riverside Hospital, and Florida Hospital. He is the husband of Joyce Berkel, who is the love of his life. He loved her so much that he devised strategies to see her even without her father's permission. He has two sons, Nigel and Dr. Ray, and is the grandfather of Emmanuel, Elijah, Raisa, and Marcus.

So what did Aubrey teach me? He helped me realize that our beloved church and our educational institutions are far from flawless regarding the racial divide. For a while the bad experiences he had shook his faith to the extent that Sabbath mornings found him at home while his family went to church. When he had the opportunity to write a paper in one of his classes, he voiced his disgust in no uncertain tones, causing the professor to squirm and to give him the lowest grade he ever received! While unfortunately some do not recover, thank God, after years of study, discussions with pastors, including his father-in-law, and prayers of a loving wife, he returned to church fellowship and is presently very active in his church. Over the years I have come to conclude that even though the church should exemplify the truths that it teaches, it is not a hotel for saints, but a hospital for sinners. I have learned that my focus should be on my Savior, "looking unto Jesus, the author and finisher of our faith" (Heb. 12:2).

Today my siblings and I form a priceless support system. We have come to experience the principle penned in Ecclesiastes 4:9–12. Verse 12 says, "Though one may be overpowered by another, two can withstand him. And a threefold cord [we may add an eightfold cord] is not quickly broken." Thank you, my dear siblings, for the contributions you made in my life, enabling me to be what I am today.

Chapter 5

The Journey to Adventism

The Man With the Lamp

One day, about a decade before Grandma Ba passed away, she saw a stranger in the village. The man was lighting a gas lamp on the steps of the dance hall, so she asked him if he was preparing for a dance. He told her that he was about to conduct a series of meetings and invited her to attend. She in turn invited her sister Aunt Minnie, and out of curiosity they both attended that opening night.

The gifted speaker was the same man lighting the gas lamp, and his name was Pastor Victor H. McEachrane. What he said was so interesting that they did not miss a night, and at the end of the series, Aunt Minnie was baptized into the Seventh-day Adventist Church. When she asked Grandma how it was that she had invited her to attend but did not accept the Bible truths, my grandmother responded, "I invited you to listen, not to join." Well, not long after that she too was baptized. The book that helped her decide, she told us, was *The Hope of the Race*.

As the evangelistic meetings continued, my mom also attended. Armed with pencil and notebook, she wrote down every Bible text the preacher quoted. Back at home, she diligently studied as if digging for hidden treasure. And when she became convinced that the Ten Commandments were still necessary, and that the seventh day was the Bible Sabbath, she obeyed the voice of the Holy Spirit and was baptized on a weekday in the city of Georgetown. But she kept it a secret from my dad.

For a time she got away with it! On Sabbath mornings we went to church, and Sabbath afternoon we were at home when Dad came home. But one Sunday morning he sat waiting for family worship and there was none! Mom had decided to have it on Sabbath mornings instead. When she told him the reason for the change, and broke the news of her baptism, Daddy was furious! I had never seen my father so angry before! He was always a quiet person, but that morning he raised his voice to such a pitch that the neighbors looked on in wonder. I was so terribly afraid that I ran downstairs!

To calm his anger, Dad left the house and took a twenty-minute walk to my grandmother's nephew to complain. Cousin Heligar later told Mom that Daddy listened quietly as he showed him the benefits of Adventism. But when he went on to tell about his smart children passing their examinations and going off to college in Trinidad, Dad's anger surfaced again. He arose and paced back and forth exclaiming, "It's the same thing I didn't want!" Unlike some fathers who couldn't wait for the children to leave home, my father wanted to see his children grow up, marry, and surround him with grandchildren. And what a household he could have, for he had nine children!

Trials and Tribulations!

As the days rolled on, peace was restored to the family and everything returned to normal. At least so it seemed to us children. Not until after his death did my mom reveal how at times Dad silently tormented her. Once he even announced that he was going to leave her. Not easily ruffled she stopped her sewing briefly to look at him and stoically replied, "The same feet you use to leave are the same feet that will bring you back!" Of course, he never really left. Whatever else transpired between our parents, no one will ever know.

But it seems that their intimacy broke down because years later a young lady appeared to tell us that she was Dad's daughter. Because of this experience, one of the seminars we now conduct in our ministry is "How to Live with a Non-Adventist Spouse" with the advice to continue your "bedroom ministry."

Mom said that at other times Daddy would refuse to give her the amount of money that he used to give before. But Mother Iris, using her God-given business acumen, always found a way to stretch what she received. She taught herself to sew and would turn a used uniform from an older sister inside out and make it look new. Mom was never delinquent in returning her tithe, and God blessed her efforts. She was able to send all of us to high school, paying our school fees, purchasing train tickets from BV to Georgetown, and keeping us looking sharp both in school and church to the extent that people often thought of us as wealthy. When Mom later revealed these things to me, I had to conclude that God is faithful in keeping His promise to "open for you the windows of heaven and pour out for you such blessing that there will not be room enough to receive it" (Mal. 3:10).

By the way, I wonder what my dad would have said if he only knew that the "Adventist saints" were also tormenting my mom. Because we lived near the public highway, traveling ministers would stop at our home first and have Mom take them around the village, especially in times of Harvest Ingathering. This angered an influential church member who was their former guide. The rumor mill was at work full time. As a result, many church members turned against Mom and her family, branding us as "stuck up" and proud. They referred to us as "dem (them) Hinds!"

If the devil was trying to discourage Mom, he did not succeed because she was determined,

Chapter 5 The Journey to Adventism

as she resolutely said, that under God, she would "allow nothing or no one to make her lose her crown." So she stuck it out, and we all continued attending church. However, as soon as the benediction was pronounced and the "Amen" said, Mom and her nine children were out the door, up the road, and home!

> *If the devil was trying to discourage Mom, he did not succeed because she was determined, as she resolutely said, that under God, she would "allow nothing or no one to make her lose her crown."*

In addition to the torment of church members, there was the torment of family members. Mom's younger sisters stopped coming to spend the summer holidays with us. Friends turned against us because we had joined "dah ting" (that thing), as Adventism was called. We felt ostracized. We were at the age when friends are important to kids, but Mother Iris kept telling us, "You don't need them! You are many, and you have each other!" Mom showed me that she knew what she believed. But even more, she knew in whom she believed. Her faith in God was always strong.

She lived to see and enjoy the fruits of her faithful labor. All her children made her proud academically. All are professionals. And spiritually, all serve the Lord and worship Him on the seventh day Sabbath. When her nest was empty, she was able to travel near and far to visit her children and grandchildren. She also reaped the benefits of being a US citizen. She lived to the ripe old age of eighty-nine, was always active, and never spent a day in the hospital!

Never Give Up!

Year after year, we prayed for our father. But despite our prayers, he seemed to have no interest in Adventism. During family worship he would sit in his recliner, and he seldom knelt with us for prayer. In spite of that we each prayed for him in his hearing. Sometimes prayers are answered immediately, but other times we have to wait. We had to wait for eighteen years!

In 1962 Pastor Oswald Edward Gordon arrived from Chicago with his lovely wife, Thelma, and three children. He became pastor of the churches in Georgetown. He had an impressive and charming personality and drove a big white Chevrolet, PAA 630, which he brought from the United States. It was the talk of the town! He soon pitched a huge tent on a big city park called Bourda Green and conducted a large evangelistic campaign. My dad had retired, and we were living in the city. To our delight, Daddy faithfully attended the meetings every night and as the truths were presented he responded to the conviction of the Holy Spirit.

As a result of these meetings, over 400 persons were baptized, and Dad was one of them! What a mighty God we serve! The new believers were organized into a brand new church called the Ephesus Church, and our family was one of those who became charter members of the vibrant new church. Mom was a church officer, I was the youth leader, and Dad became the treasurer of the church, a position he held for eight years until the time of his death! In addition, he became the accountant of the famous Davis Memorial Hospital, an Adventist institution.

Sometimes when we pray for loved ones, we wonder how long it will be before our prayers will be answered. But we do well to never give up! "And let us not grow weary while doing good, for in due season we shall reap if we do not lose heart" (Gal. 6:9). Our Savior is still in the business of saving souls! Keep on loving and keep on praying, for God still answers prayer!

Another Answered Prayer!

Mom told us that she always prayed that she would die in her sleep, and that is exactly what happened. She was living in Orlando at the time. The Sabbath before her demise she went to Patmos Church to hear her grandson Nigel play the saxophone for special music. After lunch she and her former pastor, Elder Ivan Berkell, now related by the marriage of her last son to his first daughter Joyce, sat and chatted. Among other things, they talked about the wonder and joys of heaven. On Sunday she was up at dawn as usual, had her devotion, and after breakfast was out in the sunshine taking care of her plants in the garden. On Sunday night she watched a documentary before going to bed and turned in at her usual time. Around nine o'clock Magnel went to her room to tell her that Lynette, who had spent some time with them, had safely arrived home in Michigan. She replied, "Okay." But on Monday morning, Mom did not wake up. You can imagine how shocked we all were.

I was giving final instructions to the students of my Principles of Teaching class at CUC, now University of the Southern Caribbean, when my husband, Gordon, then president of the Caribbean Union, appeared at the door of the classroom. When I saw him, I thought he had come to tell me that he had to travel for an emergency meeting. Together we walked to my office, and when I was seated, he broke the sad news. Unlike my sister Ruby who burst into loud crying at her work place, I showed no emotion. That was how Mom had wanted to die. Mom was a strong person, hardly ever sick except for hypertension, never hospitalized for any major illness. And to think of it, our loving heavenly Father had granted her request. It was good for her, although it was very difficult for us.

At the funeral my eyes filled with tears when I saw my mother lying peaceful in that casket with a dozen roses around her. I touched her hands and caressed her icy cold forehead and cheeks with my fingers—no more afraid of dead. Mom was no more. At eighty-nine years God had called her to her rest, and I believe He marks her resting place in Highland Gardens in Orlando awaiting the resurrection. By God's grace it is our desire as siblings to honor her prayer to "see all her children in the kingdom" of glory when Jesus comes again. This too is my prayer for you, my children—Esther and Marco, Sammy, John—and my siblings with their families.

There are two lessons I learned from my mother's sudden demise. First, it is good to keep in touch with loved ones in spite of busy schedules. I was too busy with the demands of teaching, visiting various churches on the island, and at times traveling abroad with my husband that I did not have time to call my mother. While it is true, I sent her birthday cards, I remember several times I ignored the gentle reminder of the Holy Spirit to call her. As a matter of fact, the very Sunday night she passed I had the nudge to call. It was about 9:00 p.m. We had just returned home from a meeting in Barbados when I felt impressed to call but did not. I knew that Mom was an "early to bed, early to rise" person, and so I decided

Chapter 5 The Journey to Adventism

to wait. I did not have the opportunity again. You can imagine how terrible I felt on the day of her funeral. It is a good thing to keep in touch with loved ones.

The second lesson I learned was that it is a good thing to let the tears flow freely. Cry as you wish, and allow yourself time to mourn. The service was indeed reassuring. My son John sang "Don't Cry for Me," and Gordon did the eulogy. At the interment we all watched as they put the last trowel of cement at the mouth of the tomb, and each one left the graveside thinking that death is real. After the repast, we returned home and indulged in chitchat, rehearsing memories of our mother laughing at both the good and the not so good. The next day I was ready to travel back home because I was scheduled to have a makeup class the following morning. You see, I prided myself that as a strong Adventist I didn't have to grieve. It would show lack of faith.

That Friday I went to class and returned to the house earlier than anticipated. It was then that I felt somewhat empty. With time on my hand and a sad yet unexplainable feeling in my heart, I attacked house cleaning with a vengeance! And the more I cleaned, the more I saw places that needed cleaning! That day I cleaned until I was exhausted. Sabbath morning I was up with the humming birds to prepare for Sabbath School. After my shower I felt empty again. There was this void that nothing was able to fill. Partly dressed, I threw myself on the bed and was lying down when Gordon came in the room and was about to say, "I thought you were ready for church." But he caught himself and instead asked, "Is it Mom?" This time the floodgates of tears opened up as I fell in his arms and cried and cried and cried some more.

I do not know how long I cried, but he held me until I could cry no more. Then I felt relieved. I continued preparing and attended the services of the day. Taking time to grieve is a good thing. Remember, Jesus wept at the grave of Lazarus. His promise still stands, "And God will wipe away every tear from their eyes; there shall be no more death, nor sorrow, nor crying. There shall be no more pain, for the former things have passed away" (Rev. 21:4). Until then I will always treasure the gem she wrote in my autograph that said,

> Life is not easy for any of us, but what of that?
>
> We must have perseverance;
>
> We must have confidence in ourselves;
>
> We must believe that we are gifted for something.
>
> And that thing, at whatever cost, must be attained.
>
> (author unknown)

Chapter 6

Tappings on My Shoulder

Early Impressions

From my early years, I could feel the hand of my Friend tapping me on my shoulder. What did He use to get my attention in my early days of my life? During childhood, Mom often attended the Anglican Church with my dad, but I went to Sunday School at the Congregational Church with Grandma Ba. I remember that I was often asked to sing and recite poems and Bible verses from memory. At times I even received monetary gifts for my effort!

Mom became a Seventh-day Adventist when I was about seven years of age, and we started to have daily morning devotions. It was difficult to get everyone together because my older siblings had to be ready to catch the train by 6:00 a.m. to travel to the city to attend high school. So my mother did an "Iris" version. We, the younger ones who attended the local public school, had to memorize the Morning Watch text for the day, be ready to say it to her correctly by eight o'clock, pray with her, then leave for school, which started at 8:30 a.m. In my last year of primary school I had a challenge because I was supposed to be at school at 8:00 a.m. But I noticed that each time I got there after eight I did not miss anything because the class did not convene. As I thought about this later, I believe that this was God introducing Himself to me.

Since childhood, reading was my passion. I read Shakespeare plays, Grimm's Fairy Tales, and others. I would browse through every book I saw, especially if it had pictures. I even had the chance to look at the pictures in my brother's medical book where I saw a picture of a fetus in the uterus. Someone promptly moved that book out of sight! So when I received the Primary Sabbath School quarterly, I enjoyed reading the Bible story for each week. One of the lessons was on the conversion of Saul. The part that intrigued me was his experience on the Damascus road, when he heard the voice saying, "Saul, Saul why do you persecute Me?"

On Sabbath afternoons after lunch, when others were sleeping, I read books such as *Patriarchs and Prophets*. The accounts of the stories fascinated me. And when I was home alone on Sabbaths because of my monthly period—we were not told why we could not attend church during menstruation—I would sing the familiar songs in the hymnal and have, as it were, my own concert. In addition to singing the tune, I used to meditate on the lyrics. One song that especially made an impact that I sang prayerfully was "Lord, I want to be a Christian."

In addition, religious art caught my attention. When I saw one of Harry Anderson's paintings of heaven and a little child with a lion with the caption, "A little child shall lead them," I envisioned myself as that child. Another favorite was the graphic painting of the angel guarding the child trying to pick a flower over the flowing stream. I learned the verse, "The angel of the Lord encamps all around those who fear Him, and delivers them" (Ps. 34:7). Truly, a picture is worth a thousand words.

Heartwarming Activities

On Sabbath afternoons we engaged in a visitation program, and this activity made a deep impression on my mind. We were placed in one of three groups—sunshine band, prayer band, and literature band. Young as I was, I was leader of a sunshine band, and we went spreading sunshine by singing, praying, and reading Scripture to any sick person to whom we were referred. I remember we visited a very sick young man laid up in bed. For several Sabbaths we ministered to him, and both he and his mother promised that when he got better he would come to our church. And we were glad to hear that. Our loving heavenly Father rewarded our efforts and the young man recovered from his illness. Sad to say he did not keep his promise to attend church. We only hope that later in life he did, and we will see him in the kingdom, when he will smilingly say, "Thank you for visiting me when I was sick."

Then there were the MV or Missionary Volunteer programs, later called AYS, now YAM, and they also inspired me. Several songs made lasting impressions on my mind. One of them was:

> Give of your best to the Master,
>
> Give of the strength of your youth
>
> Throw your soul's fresh, glowing ardor
>
> Into the battle for truth
>
> Jesus has set the example,
>
> Dauntless was He, young and brave
>
> Give Him your loyal devotion,
>
> Give Him the best that you have.
>
> (Howard B. Grose, "Give of Your Best to the Master," 1902)

Here is another one that challenged me, and it actually became a self-fulfilling prophecy!

> It may not be on the mountain's height,
>
> Or over the stormy sea
>
> It may not be at the battle's front
>
> My Lord will have need of me
>
> But if by a still, small voice He calls
>
> To paths I do not know,

I'll answer, dear Lord, with my hand in Thine,

I'll go where You want me to go.

(Mary Brown, "I'll Go Where You Want Me to Go," 1899)

And there was a third one that touched my soul as we sang it at the close of each MV meeting. It said,

Let the beauty of Jesus be seen in me

All His wonderful passion and purity

Oh, Thou Spirit divine, all my nature refine

Till the beauty of Jesus be seen in me.

(Albert Orsborn, "Let the Beauty of Jesus be Seen," 1916)

While it is true that the rhythm of those songs is slower and does not appeal to this upbeat generation, those lyrics inspired commitment to and service for God in response to His love. And so I ask, "Has our theology so greatly changed that we focus only on God's love, expecting Him to give and make us prosperous, and when He does not or delays to act, we throw a tantrum, write Him off, and claim that He does not exist?"

The MV meeting lived up to its name—Missionary Volunteer. When my older sister Lynette was MV leader at BV, we conducted a Youth for Christ evangelistic series. The youth did all the preparation, directed the nightly preliminaries, and a preached each night. I was one of them. God blessed our effort, and at the end of the campaign, four persons were baptized! One of them was a relative of one of the church members, and her twin sons joined her. I also conducted a Branch Sabbath School at our home for the neighborhood children, and Lynette helped me teach the lesson from the picture roll.

In the youth meetings, we were challenged to pursue the Bible Year reading program and read the entire Bible in one year. Since I always wanted to be first, I determined to take up the challenge. However, I didn't get very far because when I reached the "begats" with the difficult names to pronounce, I gave up the idea and never tried again until years later. Today there are several modern versions and paraphrases that make the Bible easier to understand. I encourage the young to choose a version and read the many stories that will help them to know God better.

The annual "Harvest Ingathering" was a program where we visited neighbors and friends and solicited funds to assist the church's medical, educational, and humanitarian work worldwide. I didn't like ingathering, but one year I went out with another youth. We were highly motivated when the man in the first house gave us a whole dollar! That was big money in those days! But then the donations began to shrink. Some gave us five cents, while others a quarter. After working in the hot sun, walking mile after dreary mile, we began feeling hungry pangs and decided to end our day. When we counted our coins, we had a total of $11.00, and we felt very good about it.

Spiritual Encounters

I had many friends in high school, but my best friend was Norma. I had invited her to my home for a few days, and Mom felt comfortable to allow me to go to her home in the county of Berbice. One night she had a party at her house, and even though I was tempted to dance, I did not. As the music played and the others partied, somehow my attention was drawn to the sky where the moon was beginning to pierce the dark clouds. The sight was astounding! The rays that brightened the dark clouds looked like a movie of the coming of Jesus.

Chapter 6 Tappings on My Shoulder

I visualized the description with which I was acquainted. In the distant East a dark cloud about the size of a man's hand will appear. As it draws nearer, it will become bigger and brighter. Then the trumpets of millions of angels will sound, and Jesus will appear riding on the clouds in power and great glory! What a day that will be!

As a child I liked to listen to the sermons from the pastors. Here are the punch lines of three sermons I heard that enabled me to experience encounters with God. The first was by the saintly, vision-impaired Pastor A. A. Fortune on the rebuilding of the walls by Nehemiah. His often-repeated phrase was "When the Sanballats and Tobiahs call you, say like Nehemiah, 'I am doing a great work, so that I cannot come down'" (Neh. 6:3). He referred to the Sanballats and Tobiahs as people or things that would distract us from following Jesus fully and completely. The call of commitment was to recognize them and stay away. There were tears in people's eyes as they responded to the call and came to the altar. It was a touching moment for me!

Another wakeup call came from Pastor Ivan I. Berkell, father of my sister-in-law Joyce. For his youth sermon he used Ecclesiastes 11:9. "Rejoice, O young man, in your youth, and let your heart cheer you in the days of your youth; walk in the ways of your heart, and in the sight of your eyes; but know that for all these God will bring you into judgment." The warning was clear! You can do whatever you want, live however you please, believe or not believe. But the day of reckoning is coming when all your sins will be written in the sky for all to see! So wake up and shake up, dear youth, and commit to Jesus now.

And here's one more. This was a quote from Pastor Victor H. McEachrane given on a Friday morning at Caribbean Union College. He cried, "A storm is coming—relentless in its fury! Are you prepared to meet it?" This was the same Pastor Mac who, many years before, had introduced Adventism to the people at Beterverwagting and baptized my great aunt, my grandmother Ba, and my mother. He was the first pastor of the BV SDA Church, and he visited our home often. Magnel was his favorite, and even though I was not at the age to understand most of his sermons, I remember him as the tender preacher with an appealing voice. At times tears would run down his cheeks as he preached! I believe that the Spirit of God was working on my heart, helping me to make decisions for Him even in those early teenage years.

Reality of God

One of the experiences that sealed my strong belief in the existence of God was our encounter with Lucy. She was one of the best of our home helpers. She was so good that she had privileges the others didn't have. She was even allowed to sleep on our brother's bunk bed during siesta time. What was strange about Lucy was that she did not eat the meat of any white chicken, and when asked the reason she just said that she couldn't. She also told us that she could not handle shrimp, which some neighbors would ask her to get for them when she went to market.

Suddenly the peace of the quiet afternoon was broken with Lucy screaming "I don't want to go! I don't want to go!" ...we saw her in an intense struggle with an unseen being!

Well, one memorable afternoon we started to get some answers. Lynette and I were home on school holiday, and after lunch we settled down for our siesta. Lucy did so as well. Suddenly the peace of the quiet afternoon was broken with Lucy screaming "I don't want to go! I don't want to go!" When we ran to see if she was daydreaming, we saw her in an intense struggle with an unseen being! She was dead serious, and tears ran down her cheeks. When we called to her and she did not answer, my sister told me to go and call her relatives. In the meantime Lyn began playing hymns on the piano, which quieted her. The hymns continued until I returned with the relative. By then she was sitting on the bed. The struggle was over, but she was in a dazed condition.

Several days later, Lucy told us that because of severe poverty her mother had sold her to "people of the underworld." She said that every morning she would find under a tree enough money to take care of their needs for the day. In exchange, she had to serve them by heeding certain restrictions. For example, she could not eat the flesh of a white chicken or handle shrimp and crabs. If she did, they would take her away. Because she had disobeyed, they had come to take her away! No wonder she was struggling and crying, "I don't want to go!" As strange as it might seem, this is a true account of what happened that afternoon because I was an eyewitness. This experience confirmed my belief in the reality of Satan. And if the devil exists, surely God does too!

Mom also told me a story that sends chills up my spine as I reflect on it. One of Dad's coworkers tried to get rid of him because he wanted his position. So he went to a spirit medium, whom we called the "obeah man," to ask him to do the job. When the rival mentioned my dad's name to the necromancer, he bluntly refused by saying, "You want me to do that to Mr. Hinds? I can't do such a thing. He is a good man, and I won't hurt him for anything!" He later told this to my mom, advising her to alert Daddy to beware of that coworker. It is alleged that the same thing happened to my mother-in-law Maisie, which resulted in her illness for many years. Someone hurt the wife in order to get at the husband because he wanted his position. I met her once and found her to be a sweet, hospitable lady. The work of demonic forces is nothing new. King Saul visited the witch of Endor. You can read this sad story in 1 Samuel 28.

Here's one more story of my Friend's tap upon my shoulder. I was teaching at Tutorial High School at the time and staying at the home of "Lady P" who is now my sister-in-law. As I got home one afternoon, I heard an inner voice said, "Pray for your dad." He was returning from his paid vacation in England, during which time he proudly gave Thelma in holy wedlock to George Cadogan. And like the apostle Paul, "I was not disobedient to the heavenly vision." So I knelt by my bedside and prayed a simple but earnest prayer for my dad. When he returned to Guyana, he told us about a violent storm and shipwreck off the coast of Portugal and of their abandoning the ship in small boats in the rough waters. They were then put on a plane to complete the trip, and they had experienced turbulence in the sky. He was terribly afraid. The shipwreck occurred on the same day that I had been impressed to pray. And so I learned that as long as your heart is tuned to God's heart, whenever you feel impressed to do something, do it!

These incidents during my early years taught me that God is eagerly searching for us, and He uses simple experiences to draw us to Him. He declares, "Yes, I have loved you with an everlasting love; therefore with lovingkindness I have drawn you" (Jer. 31:3). And when we feel Him tugging at our hearts, if we would just only stop and fall into His arms, we would feel His loving embrace and hear the throb of His heart as He whispers, "I love you. I will lead you. Just follow Me." It's very true that "Christ is constantly working upon the heart. Little by little ... impressions are made that tend to draw the souls to Christ. These may be received through meditating on Him, through reading the Scriptures, or through hearing the word from the living preacher" (White, *The Desire of Ages*, p. 172).

Chapter 7

In Hot Pursuit!

High School Years

In the final year of primary school, promising students were given the opportunity to attend the most prestigious high schools operated by the British expatriates. Success at their qualifying exam meant a four-year scholarship. For girls it was Bishops High, for boys Queens College. Even though the exam was on Sabbath, Mom allowed me to go. The exam consisted of English, math, and an interview where among others each applicant was questioned about their father's work, religion, etc. I knew I did well and was sure of acceptance. However, when we received the much-anticipated letter, our hopes were dashed because it was not good news for me. I just could not answer the question why. However, in retrospect, I firmly believe that Bishops High School was not in God's plan for me then or ever.

Although deeply disappointed, I succeeded at the end of primary school examination and was content to attend one of the leading private high schools in the country—Tutorial High School. Regardless of the school one attended, Seventh-day Adventism was very unpopular in those days. It was considered a cult. People made fun of Adventists calling them "Seven Days," or "Seven Devils!" One day our classroom teacher, who was also our Bible teacher and a devout Catholic, decided that the class needed to have a picnic. The day she suggested was a Saturday. Before I could say anything, I

Chapter 7 In Hot Pursuit!

was surprised to hear my classmates say, "Miss, we can't have it on Saturday, Waveney won't be able to come. She is 'Seven Days'!"

What impressed me was that their words were not said in the usual derogatory way that adults did but in the caring tones of my classmates! I learned that being "Seven Days" was not such a bad thing after all. It earned me the love and respect of my classmates. At present the Seventh-day Adventist Church is one of the fastest growing churches and has over 18 million members in more than 200 countries of the world. It operates the largest Protestant educational as well as health care system in the world. And it is one of largest religions in Guyana and the Caribbean.

In high school I continued to diligently study. I knew how to put study time above playtime. I remember setting aside one Sunday morning to study the Pythagorean theorem line by line until I mastered it. I know about staying up past midnight to conquer quadratic equations and calculus. After that, math was no problem for me. I made good grades, and I was almost always at the top of my class.

High school days were pleasant days as well as innocent days. We were so innocent that one day in class when the words "sexual intercourse" tumbled out of the mouth of one of my friends we were ignorant of the meaning! The teacher overheard and asked her if she knew what she had just said, to which her answer was "No." Apparently she had heard it from someone and nonchalantly had mouthed the word in class. Anyhow, he stopped the class to explain. But I honestly do not recall what he said, except that we should refrain from using those words in public. I had a group of special friends with whom I traveled on the train, and each day we walked a few miles from Kitty Station to school and back. Those who did not travel but lived near the train station joined us at the station and walked along with us. It was fun, and I really enjoyed my high school days.

When I was in Form Two, I was chosen to reply to a letter from a girl from the United States who was desirous of having Guyanese pen pals. When I sent off the first letter, she replied and sent her picture. She was a white girl from Birmingham, Alabama. But when I reciprocated by sending her my picture, I never heard from her again! And that happened to my other classmates as well. At that time we did not know about the ugly phantom of racism that plagued America. Our country had benefitted from Britain's Emancipation Act of 1833 three decades before the abolition of slavery in the United States. And since our black population was in the vast majority, we did not suffer the horrors of racism. So her rejection was of no consequence to me.

For the next two years I continued to study to prepare for the end of high school exam, which was the British Senior Cambridge examination. The Sabbath before the exam I engaged in a complete fast, neither eating nor drinking from sundown on Friday until sundown on Sabbath. The focus of my prayer was that God would bring to my memory what I had studied. That Monday morning I approached each of the six subjects—English, math, Latin, French, history, and economics—with confidence, knowing that my God was with me. When the results were published, I was successful in five, and needed just a few more marks to pass economics. I still thought I did very well in that subject since we had no textbooks and it was introduced only two quarters before the exam. I gave thanks to God, for He had truly come through for me.

Young and Restless!

After being successful at the Senior Cambridge exam with a Grade 2, I continued to study at the same high school in order to write the Higher Senior Cambridge examination. If I was successful, I would have another chance to attend that prestigious Bishops High for girls. I did Latin, history, and general paper. But even though we went to class every day, the principal had no time to teach us, and we were actually on our own. Instead, he had us substitute for any absent teacher in the lower classes.

I did so well in teaching and managing an unruly class to which I was often assigned that I was employed as a full-time teacher after my exam. I was asked to teach French, Latin, and history in four Forms. The school had three campuses, and I was appointed assistant to the principal with the responsibility for female affairs on all of the campuses. When I met with the female teachers on staff, we identified some needs of the girls in the school, decided on implementation, and reported to the principal. Administration readily agreed to some of the ideas, and I was given the task to talk to the girls of each form. In addition, I served as vice principal of one of the branches of about 200 students.

As a member of the school's Sports Committee, I learned the power of the will. They had planned a dance as a fundraiser, and as a responsible member, and the one responsible for the girls, I needed to attend. But as an Adventist, I was determined that I would not yield to the temptation to dance. So I requested to be in charge of the soft drinks. Do you know that even though I was approached several times by some admiring young men for a dance, this nineteen year old graciously refused their offer? In our seminars we teach the "Equation of Victory"—"I choose + I pray = I can!" The apostle James says, "Resist the devil and he will flee from you. Draw near to God and He will draw near to you" (James 4:7, 8). And Joshua tells us, "Choose for yourselves this day whom you will serve … But as for me and my house, we will serve the Lord" (Joshua 24:15). Whatever you make up your mind to do, you can do it!

I worked at Tutorial High for about three and a half years and simply loved it. I was thrilled to see the eyes of the children light up and big smiles spread across their faces when they understood a concept and were able to translate the sentence from English to French correctly. I can still remember one of the Form 2 boys looking intently at me one morning before class and blurting out, "You know, Miss, you are a nice teacher!" It seemed that I was at Tutorial to stay for a long while, but God had other plans that He soon revealed.

The devil was also on hand trying to lure me away. A dear cousin, Clayton, invited Maisie and me to join his group and learn to play basketball. His father was appointed accountant of another branch of Bookers Sugar Estates about the same time as my dad was. In addition, his sister Peggy was my very best friend in primary school. Since it was good recreation, we went every Sunday afternoon. After we had learned to play the game, he invited an experienced girls' team from the city to play against us. And of course, they beat us badly every time. As the spies reported to Moses, they were giants, and we were like pygmies! But in spite of the losses, we cherished the experience.

After the game he invited all for refreshments at his home. During this time we chatted with each other with background music. When they played a favorite calypso, they increased the volume and that encouraged us to pair off and dance. And as I said before, I loved to dance! That soon became the norm, every Sunday after practice or after a game, we got together and we danced. But at two different times I sprained my ankle and could not play or dance. Evidently God was trying to gain my

Chapter 7 In Hot Pursuit!

attention, but I surely was not listening. That activity blossomed into the idea of having a big party with more friends, music and dancing. And I was planning to attend! But God had His eyes on me!

Full Surrender!

On the Sabbath just before the big party, I attended a youth rally at the Georgetown Church, the largest church in the country, and Elder B. L. Archbold, president of Caribbean Union College, was the main speaker. His topic, "Untamed Youth," was taken from the billboard of a cinema. And in his electrifying sermon, he talked about the various things in which the youth in the world were engaged and how these were creeping into the church. He targeted the cinema, sexual intimacy, and dancing. My Friend was having an awesome, face to face encounter with me!

I can hardly remember the rest of that sermon! All I know is that it had such a profound impact on me, as well as other "untamed youth" who were "young and restless," that I responded to the call, went up to the altar, and reconsecrated my life to God. That was the day the Holy Spirit gave His direct appeal: "Waveney, give Me your heart. Serve Me fully." I gladly surrendered, and with the others I sang the AY theme song:

> We have heard Your call Lord Jesus
>
> And our hearts respond with joy;
>
> We will pledge You our allegiance
>
> And Your truth our tongues employ.
>
> The youth of the world for the Man of Galilee!
>
> The youth of the world from all sin and self set free;
>
> Every talent pledged in service now and through eternity,
>
> The youth of the world for the Man of Galilee!

I had made a full surrender! From that decisive moment, party going, basketball playing, and dancing were all over for me! Recently I heard a preacher say, "God likes to chase after sinners." He surely was in hot pursuit of me, and I thank Him that I didn't leave Him running out of breath. I stopped, turned, looked into His loving face, and placed my hand in His and said, "Take my life and let it be consecrated Lord to Thee." That was my hour of decision. It gave direction to my life.

> *"God likes to chase after sinners." He surely was in hot pursuit of me, and I thank Him that I didn't leave Him running out of breath.*

I am glad that after many years with Jesus, I have no regrets. I missed neither the dancehall nor the movie theatre because Jesus became my all in all, just as the hymn title "Jesus is the Joy of Living" states. The eminent C.S. Lewis, the one-time atheist, agrees with me. Speaking of his conversion in 1931, he says he "was surprised by joy!" So what are you waiting for? "O, taste and see that the Lord is good!"

After that life-changing program, Mom and I stayed to meet President Archbold because he knew my sister Cynthia. When he learned of my desire to attend CUC, he told me he would send a student to talk with me, but that student never came. I probably would not have been able to attend at that time anyhow because Lynette was at CUC and Rudolph at Oakwood. Mom suggested that I wait until after Lyn graduated.

Meanwhile I continued to teach at Tutorial and joined a money saving plan that we called "sou-sou." It involved putting your money each month for a number of months in one pool that is held by a trusted individual and getting the accumulated amount in a lump sum when your turn came around. It really caused us to save intentionally. So I saved and I waited to attend CUC. How was I to know that this was all in God's plan for me and that He was working according to His timetable? You will soon know!

Part Two:

Love, Marriage, and Ministry

Chapter 8

Intersecting Pathways

Here and There

I lived in the same pastoral district, not in the same village as Gordon. I lived at BV, and he lived at Buxton about five miles away. Because of the proximity of the two churches, the pastor would bring the two churches together for combined youth activities. One such activity was a picnic at BV backlands, and to get there, the young people had to travel by boat. On the return trip this young man and I happened to be in the same broad bottomed boat. We engaged in a game of marble checkers, and the game eventually came down to two players—this good-looking guy from Buxton and me. We made move after move, and to my surprise, I emerged the winner! I didn't even know his name even though I did take note of his good looks. But at that time I had a high school boyfriend.

Later on, we met again when our pastor scheduled rehearsals for a play called "The Enchanted Shirt," in which we both participated. He was the page and I was a fairy. We met again the Sunday morning of our baptism. He was seated in the front seat of the car when Pastor O. C. Walker stopped for my sister and me to take us to the city church where we were baptized on the same day.

Years after Mission Youth Director Adrian T. Westney challenged the various MV societies to participate in a countrywide music competition. The leader of the winning choir would be a delegate to the upcoming General Conference Youth Convention to be held in Cuba.

Chapter 8 Intersecting Pathways

Choirs from Buxton, BV, and other societies participated. And there he was again—in the Buxton choir! Under Lynette's leadership, the BV won outright, and she was chosen as the delegate. We had a large and well-organized choir, and when we stood up to sing—girls in white and pink, and boys in black pants and white shirts—the electrified audience cheered! Clement Texeira, who later married Gordon's sister Dolly, was the only bass voice. After that, it was years later before our paths crossed again. And here is how.

My grown brothers and sisters had left the Hinds nest at BV to study abroad—England, the United States, and Trinidad—leaving Ruby, Aubrey, and I. So we moved to Enmore where my father was an accountant. This senior position came with a lot of privileges—a large house in a gated compound, free travel in a chauffeured van that took us to school in the city, 6 percent off purchases at Bookers Stores, and a gardener who planted flowers and vegetables. It was he who introduced us to cauliflower.

> *My dad was so respected by the staff that one night when we appeared at a function, everyone in the club stood to their feet when he entered the hall!*

My dad was so respected by the staff that one night when we appeared at a function, everyone in the club—they were mostly white expatriates from England—stood to their feet when he entered the hall! I cannot tell you how proud I was of my dad and how I savored the moment! No wonder they did so! He computed their taxes, and he found the errors amidst the maze of figures when they could not balance the books. Mom told us that at times while in bed she would hear him doing calculations as he figured the problem in his head. He was a man of professional integrity.

Getting Nearer

Everything was in our favor because we could use the van on Sabbaths to attend our church at BV in the morning and return home in the afternoon. Ruby, Aubrey, and I were living in luxury with Mom and Dad. But as the saying goes, "All good things must come to an end." Firstly, I could no longer travel on the van to school because I was a teacher and no longer a student. So God opened the home of "Lady P" who lived in the city, and my sister Magnel and I stayed there. Secondly, we could no longer use the van on Sabbaths because the fun-loving young expatriates wanted to get their entertainment in the city on Saturday nights, and the driver and the van needed to "rest" on Saturday. We had to find another way to get from Enmore to the church in Beterverwagting. So Dad hired a private vehicle.

One Sabbath morning the vehicle did not show up. So Mom decided that we would walk the two miles to get to the main road and use public transportation. It was late, and our mother hated to be late! So as we neared Buxton on our way to BV, she said, "We will not get to BV in time for Sabbath School, so let's stop at Buxton, where the church is not far from the main highway." And that's just what we did. The church at Buxton was small, with just a few members, and fewer young people.

I don't remember what happened at Sabbath School, but I remember that at the worship service Roy McGarrell did the intercessory prayer and Gordon Martinborough was the speaker. I do not recall the sermon title, but I remember his stirring introduction. It was quoted from a hymn: "Hushed was the evening hymn, the temple courts were dark, The lamp was burning dim before the sacred ark, When suddenly a voice divine rang through the silence of the shrine!" And with the serious tone of his voice, it was an attention getter indeed! Ruby and I joked about it for a long time after. The sermon was indeed a blessing, especially since it was coming from a youth like myself. It was then I heard for the first time that God has a plan for every life, and we need to ask Him to reveal that plan to us.

We kept attending that church for some time, and I was asked to join the Roy, Shirley, and Gordon trio to make it a quartet. One afternoon on our return home from church, Cynthia, my eldest sister who was home on vacation, predicted that one of these days Mom would hear a knock on her door and Gordon, who was unattached (Roy and Shirley were engaged), would be standing there asking for permission to date either Ruby or me.

To me, her prediction was out of the realm of reality, because in those days it was believed that young ministers were looking for girls of fair complexion with long straight hair and could play the piano or sing solos, and I possessed none of these qualifications. More than that, he did not seem to be interested in girls, much less in marriage. He was focused on his goal of becoming a minister. Then in September 1959 there was a lovely farewell ceremony, which I helped Sister Agatha Mosely (recently deceased at ninety-four) to organize. Soon after that the trio left for CUC.

Meeting Again!

Mom, Ruby, and I continued to attend the Buxton Church. While there I started the Buxton Pathfinder Club for the few teenagers, and among them was Dolly Martinborough. Vashti Hinds was my helper, and when we realized we needed materials, we decided to meet one afternoon after school and visit the mission office in the city. There we met Youth Director Adrian T. Westney. He greeted us and began to question me about my educational goals, my work, and my achievements. When he learned that I had a Grade 2 Senior Cambridge Certificate, he told me of an elementary teacher training program that was scheduled to begin in January at Caribbean Union College and offered me a two-year tuition paid scholarship in exchange for four years of work with the Guyana Mission upon my return. I could not believe it! I left his office in serious contemplation.

Lady P, at whose home I stayed during the week, thought it was a good offer, but she told me to pray about it. Mom and Dad also endorsed the offer, but they reminded me of my obligation to the mission for four years. After much prayer I felt God had made the way for me, and I decided to seize the opportunity. So three months after Gordon arrived at CUC, I too descended on the college campus ready to begin the program in January 1960! At that time my sister Lyn was in her final year there. But why did I end up at CUC then and not before? Because, having given my life to my Best Friend, I came under the direction of His guiding hand!

Many years later I learned from my sister's friend Norma that Pastor Westney had his eye on me for a long time. He was impressed with the way I took initiative, doing what needed to be done when we were stranded in the forest on the trip to Kaieteur Falls where like Jacob of old the ground was our bed, the stars our canopy, and a stone our pillow. Thank God the weather was kind and there was no rain that night. At that time he told her that I was a good candidate for CUC and that he would do whatever he could to get me there, and that was his opportune moment!

Chapter 9

Love Is in the Air!

"Happy Birthday!"

Since the day I made a full surrender to the love of my Friend Jesus through the preaching of Elder Archbold, I dreamed of going to CUC. Finally, my dream had become a reality! The first year of college was uneventful. I made friends with Grace Ward (now Grace Van Lange) and others. For most of my college years, I lived in Room 2, and in a sense, I mothered two teenagers, Bertha needed to be urged to get out of bed and go to her morning class and Floricita needed answers to questions on anything she heard and did not understand. After "lights out," she would stand by my bed and say, "Miss Hinds, why …" Only when she was satisfied with the answer did she go to bed.

> *"Lord, today is my birthday, and once again I am recommitting my life to You. And today, I want You to show me which of these two young men is the one You have chosen for me. Let the one You have chosen tell me 'Happy Birthday.'"*

In the mornings, after my teenage roommates left for class, I took the time to commune with my Friend. On my birthday, September 21, 1960, I prayed a specific prayer that was like this, "Lord, today is my birthday, and once again I am recommitting my life to You. And today, I want You to show me which of these two young men is the one You have chosen for me. Let the one You have chosen tell me 'Happy Birthday.' And if perchance marriage is not in Your plan for me, show me where You would have me work for You." I was echoing the sentiments of a hymn we liked to sing:

> It may not be on the mountain's height,
>
> Or over the stormy sea;
>
> It may not be at the battle's front
>
> My Lord will have need of me.
>
> But if by a still, small voice He calls
>
> To paths I do not know,
>
> I'll answer, dear Lord, with my hand in Thine,
>
> I'll go where you want me to go.
>
> (Mary Brown, "I'll Go Where You Want Me to Go," 1899)

At that time there was an education student and a ministerial student who wanted to marry me immediately after his graduation that year. As a matter of fact, he knelt on the lawn saying "I love you" in front of all assembled, including the president. Like weak-faithed Gideon, I put my fleece on the floor and asked God for a sign. But strangely enough, I heard nothing from either of the two, although they both knew it was my birthday!

But someone else did say "Happy birthday!" That morning my pre-lunch class was canceled because the teacher had an emergency. Instead of returning to the dorm, a couple of us decided to visit a friend at her new apartment, then get to the dining room early. Soon there was a knock on the door, and since I was the one nearest the door, I was asked to open it. There stood Gordon Martinborough! And he said, "Happy birthday!" But somehow it did not register that this was the answer to my prayer because I was not expecting the greeting from him!

> *Soon there was a knock on the door, and since I was the one nearest the door, I was asked to open it. There stood Gordon Martinborough! And he said, "Happy birthday!"*

It is true that we had known each other since the Buxton years. And it is true that we were classmates in the first year class of Bible Doctrines. In every test he scored full points except one time when the results were posted on the board, and there were two persons with full points! Everyone knew that Gordon was one of them, but who was the other person? Yes, it was one of the teacher trainees named Waveney!

The Proposal

In the last quarter of my first year, my parents appeared on the college campus. They were on their way to one of the islands of the Caribbean for vacation when they had to change their plans. Upon request, they were permitted to stay on campus with us. Mom stayed with us in the ladies' dorm, and they found a place for my dad in the men's dorm. Ironically, the only available space was in Gordon's room! Now Mom had known Gordon

Chapter 9 Love Is in the Air!

from attending Buxton Church, but my dad had not met him before. Was this coincidence or providence? Gordon counted it as a God-given sign. Dad was so impressed with him that when he later asked for my hand in marriage, according to my dad, "I gave him the green light!" We joke about it almost every time we are fortunate to have green lights perpetually on the highway.

We were now in the second year of college. The class was Christian Education, and once again Gordon and I were in the same class. Because of lack of classroom space, this class met once a week on Friday mornings in the dining room. One morning in class Gordon sat at a desk right in my view so that every time I raised my head I had to see him. Then surprisingly, after class he waited for me and asked for a "date" at the home of a faculty member that Saturday night. It was there that he told me of his love for me since meeting back home, but that he was unsure then because at that time I did not seem to be the spiritually mature girl that would make a good minister's wife.

I made him wait for a week before giving him an answer! Why? Because I needed time to think and pray. The truth is that I had forgotten all about that "Happy birthday" prayer request to God my Father. I spoke to my best friend Grace. She told me that I had to be sure because he was one of the serious guys, and she encouraged me to pray. And when I told my eldest sister Cynthia she said, "What did you say?" She probably remembered her prophecy. By the end of the week I was sure, and when we met again I said, "Yes!" Gordon later told me that it was the happiest moment of his life!

Not long after we met again at the home of the college pastor and head of the theology department, and Gordon slipped a "diamond" on my finger! Strangely, we did not seal our commitment with a kiss. How could we do so in the home of a faculty member when CUC was so strict in regards to male-female relationships? Little did we know that the pastor and his wife would have welcomed it, but they said nothing to encourage it, and we did nothing to jeopardize our standing in their eyes. Even now, I fondly remember and savor the moment.

More importantly, I sealed my commitment to him one Sabbath afternoon on our return from San Fernando. We had hired a car for the day to visit my eldest sister Cynthia who was teaching at the high school there. With us were Gordon's best friend, Roy, and his sister, Shirley, who had been engaged even before they had left for college. As I thought of the future as a minister's wife and realized that ministers were often assigned here, there, and everywhere, I felt moved to tell him that I would go with him wherever he was sent. I am happy to say that the commitment has stayed with me over the years, carrying me through the vicissitudes or "curve balls" of the ministry for over fifty years. So I endorse the fact that "God never leads His children otherwise than they would choose to be led, if they could see the end from the beginning, and discern the glory of the purpose which they are fulfilling as co-workers with Him" (White, *The Desire of Ages,* pp. 224, 225).

No More Meat!

Three months after experiencing the pomp and splendor of graduation and writing the qualifying teachers' examination, I returned to Guyana and started teaching at the Adventist elementary school in the city. I was responsible for grades 1 to 3, and when the principal had to leave, I was asked to take her place.

One day I overheard Papa Marts (my fond name for my future father-in-law), asking Mom, "Do you think Waveney will continue the non meat diet that she had at CUC?" Then as if answering his own question, he continued, "I don't think she will!" And he was right! I could not wait to sink my teeth into the succulent beef steak served with potatoes or the chicken curry and rice.

At home we were not vegetarians. We didn't even know that word until Cynthia had returned from college on vacation and made "drumsticks" from flour. We watched her make the dough, wash out the starch to get the gluten, season it, form it, boil it, then fry it and insert the stick, and serve it. Even though we were skeptical, we all enjoyed this delicious meat substitute. However, when she returned to college, the gluten experiment went with her! We went back to eating steak, chicken, and fish. When I was at CUC, students often ate meat while visiting off-campus relatives, and Lyn and I got our share by visiting San Fernando.

Although I ate meat for many years, three things happened that caused me to become a vegetarian. First, Mom and I saw a diseased cow, and we imagined it on its way to the slaughterhouse and then to our plate. So we scratched it off our weekly menu and decided to use chicken instead. Every Friday Mom purchased two birds, and I had the task of cleaning the carcasses. Over time the weekly handling and cleaning of the birds negatively affected me, and as a result, I turned away from that as well. Was my Friend preparing me for the future? Just recently I learned from a noted cardiologist that chicken has more cholesterol than red meat! And the buildup of cholesterol plaque in the arteries can cause a heart attack.

The third thing that happened to cause a diet change was a Sabbath School lesson. We discovered that the original menu designed by the Creator Himself was a plant-based diet, and it was only after the flood when all vegetation was destroyed that meat was added to man's diet. We also noted the physical benefits of a non-meat diet as evidenced in the story of the youthful prophet Daniel (Dan. 1). What we studied made such an impact on my dad that he too joined us in our "no meat diet." With Dad on board, we were now vegetarians. And all this happened before my wedding!

So Papa Marts, you were not right after all! Since our marriage vows over fifty years ago, we have continued our vegetarian diet. Even today, our daughter Esther is unashamed to declare her plant-based food choice when she has company. Occasionally we use a piece of fish, and especially when we are traveling and vegetarian meals are not available. But otherwise we follow a plant-based diet, which today's health professionals agree is the best option.

Papa Marts

Let me tell you more about my father-in-law, Papa Marts. I found him quite interesting. He had a kind of half smile, spoke slowly with peculiar hand gestures, and rolled his eyes at different times when he spoke. And he could engage you in conversation for a long time. That's exactly what he did one Sabbath after the worship service at the Buxton Church. He told me about his life and about his wife and how he had prayed to get her. He told me about his accident and how the physician told him he would never walk again because his back was broken. Then one day he felt the urge to get up from his hospital bed, and when he made that move, he found that miraculous healing had taken place! How thankful he was to God! As he talked, I wondered why he was telling me these things and preventing me from having my lunch. Maybe he had me in mind for his son, but Gordon was not on my mind!

Chapter 9 Love Is in the Air!

He had gone off to CUC. But then you know how shrewd the elderly can be. Maybe he knew more than we did.

He also taught me to save for the children even when they were very small. When Esther was still a baby, he stayed with us to recuperate from major surgery. The day he left he gave me a bank book with the name "Esther Martinborough" on it and $5.00 in the account he had started! He told me to try to add a little every month. He did the same for Samuel when he was born. I followed his advice and continued to save. However, not long after we left for California, he passed away, and when we returned to Guyana, I was told that since the account had his signature, I could not access it. I learned that the signature on an account is very important.

Papa Marts used to say that there was one hymn he did not like to sing because it said, "Lord I care not for riches neither silver nor gold," and that was not true for him. He cared about riches and wished he had silver and gold. The hymn he preferred was "A Child of the King," in which the lyrics talk about the riches of our heavenly Father:

> My Father is rich in houses and lands,
>
> He holdeth the wealth of the world in His hands!
>
> Of rubies and diamonds, of silver and gold,
>
> His coffers are full, He has riches untold.
>
> I'm a child of the King,
>
> A child of the King;
>
> With Jesus my Savior,
>
> I'm a child of the King.
>
> (Harriet E. Buell, 1877)

Indeed those lyrics affirm our identity. Any youth who personally affirms "I'm a child of the King" is likely to have a positive self worth, and less likely to engage in harmful activities to enhance his/her self esteem.

It is interesting to observe that my dad and Papa Marts passed away within one month of each other. Papa Marts spent one night in the hospital. We later learned that not long before he was with Roy and Shirley and had enjoyed an ice cream cone. We were shocked to hear of his passing. My dad, on the other hand, spent one week in the hospital with a stomach ailment, and day by day we were updated on his condition. On Friday he told Magnel, the nursing administrator of the hospital, that "he was packed and ready." He passed away that Friday afternoon. The next Sabbath morning while attending the La Sierra Church I could not hold back the tears as I remembered that just the week before he was in the Ephesus Church and now his seat was vacant. We were penniless in California and could not make the trip home to celebrate their lives at the service. We await the resurrection!

Love Notes

During the two years between graduation and marriage, Gordon and I exchanged love letters. Here is a verse of one of the poems he composed and sent to me. It's entitled "My Moonlight."

> Sweet Waveney, I'm thinking of you tonight,
>
> As I stand and look at the bright moonlight;
>
> Somehow, sweetheart, as I gaze at its grace,
>
> I think of the lovely smile of your face;
>
> And in that sweet peace, I'm in ecstasy

Like the moments when you are right beside me!

For you are my moonlight, my love!

But while my earthly lover was sending me love notes, my heavenly Lover and Friend was also tugging at my heart. One holiday morning a few months before our wedding, I was lying in bed meditating and paging through Ellen White's masterpiece on the life of Christ, *The Desire of Ages*. As I turned the pages my eyes rested on the chapter "Gethsemane," and I started reading the opening paragraph. My interest peaked when I read the second paragraph: "And what was to be gained by this sacrifice? How hopeless appeared the guilt and ingratitude of men! In its hardest features Satan pressed the situation upon the Redeemer: The people who claim to be above all others ... have rejected You.... One of Your own disciples ... will betray You. One of Your most zealous disciples will deny You. All will forsake You" (p. 687).

Satan had come for the last fearful struggle. I never knew that the conflict was so terrible. In essence the tempter was telling Jesus that He didn't have to go to the cross, He could return to heaven and leave man to suffer their own penalty for their sins. The fate of humanity trembled in the balance. The prophet continued, "But now the history of the human race comes up before the world's Redeemer.... He beholds its impending fate, and His decision is made. He will save man at any cost to Himself.... And He will not turn from His mission.... His prayer now breathes only submission: 'If this cup may not pass away from Me, except I drink it, Thy will be done'" (pp. 690, 693).

"O my God!" I silently exclaimed. It was another sobering moment, another life-changing experience for me. I could identify with Rusty Goodman who asked, "Who am I that a King would bleed and die for? Who am I that He would pray 'Not My will but Thine' for? The answer I may never know why He ever loved me so That to an old rugged cross He'd go for who am I?"

That morning with tears in my eyes I surrendered my life to God for service. He had made Himself known to me, and I wanted to follow Him.

That morning with tears in my eyes I surrendered my life to God for service. He had made Himself known to me, and I wanted to follow Him. He was preparing me for a life of ministry and dedicated service in the days and years ahead. *The Desire of Ages* became my companion as it revealed to me the life story and love story of Jesus. My constant prayer was "Thank you, Father, for sending Jesus; thank you, Jesus, for bearing it all for me." Here is useful counsel, "It would be well for us to spend a thoughtful hour each day in contemplation of the life of Christ. We should take it point by point, and let the imagination grasp each scene, especially the closing ones. As we thus dwell upon His great sacrifice for us, our confidence in Him will be more constant, our love will be quickened, and we shall be more deeply imbued with His spirit" (*The Desire of Ages*, p. 83).

I was now receiving two types of love letters, and I was experiencing a double love story. I had a human lover. But even better, I had a divine Lover! And with the apostle John, I could exclaim, "Behold what manner of love" (1 John 3:1)!

Chapter 10

Here Comes the Bride!

Two years at CUC had come and gone, and I was back in Guyana to satisfy my part of the scholarship—four years of work for two years of tuition. I had left single and returned engaged to be married to someone I least expected. God's dealings with humans never cease to amaze me. On January 1962 I began teaching at the Adventist primary school in Georgetown. In this one-room school, there were about 100 students with three teachers to manage grades one to five, and chalkboards to separate the classes. I had about forty children in grades one to three, and later that year I was also asked to be principal. God blessed my efforts, and the enrollment increased to about 130 with two more teachers. In addition, our fundraising Christmas concert raised enough money for us to start a small school library, and we adjusted the government curriculum to include our religious activities.

Wedding of the Year!

While I was teaching, Gordon was pastoring a district of six churches on the West Coast of Berbice, about three hours by train from the city. In those days there was no cell phone, e-mail, or Skype, so we depended on letters to keep the love fire burning. This was a continuation of how it was done when we were students at college. While at CUC the leaders monitored male-female interaction like an eagle hovering over its chicks to protect them from predators. Men and women could never meet except on Saturday nights for dinners, marches, progressive hikes, or visits in the ladies' parlor for those with a high GPA or in the home of a faculty member. Consequently, each Friday afternoon we penned our letters of love in prose or poetry and sent them by a trusted mail carrier. So back in Guyana, we again depended on the mail. At times Gordon was able to visit me in Georgetown, and when he did he would bring his favorite gift—a bar of "Cadbury chocolate" with nuts in it. We still smile at the memory.

At 5:15 p.m. on Wednesday, April 17, 1963, the organ struck the chord of the bridal march, and the entrance of the bridal party and the flower girl announced to the anxious groom and the waiting crowd that the bride had arrived.

For the Seventh-day Adventist Church in the city of Georgetown, it was the wedding of the year! At 5:15 p.m. on Wednesday, April 17, 1963, the organ struck the chord of the bridal march, and the entrance of the bridal party and the flower girl announced to the anxious groom and the waiting crowd that the bride had arrived. There she was as radiant as ever, leaning on the arms of her proud father, stepping to the rhythm of "Here Comes the Bride." Then before Pastors Oswald E. Gordon and Milton E. Neblett, our parents, and a large number of relatives, friends and well-wishers, Gordon and I committed to each other for "better or worse, richer or poorer, in sickness or health until death do us part." Our hearts thrilled to the music of "O Perfect Love":

O perfect Love, all human thought transcending,

Lowly we kneel in prayer before thy throne,

That theirs may be the love which knows no ending,

Whom thou in sacred vow dost join in one.

(Dorothy Gurney, 1883)

One strange phrase of the prayer that I still remember is, "Give them enough tears to make them tender." I think that through the years God answered that prayer.

Strange Honeymoon!

After the reception, we spent the night at a hotel before traveling to the town of McKenzie, now Linden, for our honeymoon. Then early the next morning we boarded the boat called "RH Carr," climbed to the top deck which was reserved for us, and traveled the sixty-five miles up the Demerara River in style and comfort. My husband's thoughtfulness then and now continue to make me feel very special!

Our honeymoon suite was a lovely room overlooking the river, and it was breezy and romantic. Among other things, we discussed plans for the future. We also read the book *Happiness for Husbands and Wives*, which took the place of the marriage counseling that we never had. In addition, we enjoyed a speedboat ride further up the river. And here's something else. Gordon conducted a week of prayer for the McKenzie Church! That surely wasn't planned as a honeymoon activity! But political problems in the country escalated, causing a total shutdown. All workers went on strike, crippling the country for ninety days! Since their pastor was stranded in the city and we had an extended honeymoon in his district, the members asked Gordon to help instead of canceling the program, especially at this time when we needed to pray.

As the days dragged on, we got more and more anxious to get back to the city and set up our first home. We wanted to face the realities of married life. So we took the chance to travel on one of the launches that temporarily replaced the ferry. It was providential that we did that sooner rather than later. Eventually river travel became so dangerous that two church members lost their lives when on one trip the launch was blown up! As we look back upon it, our honeymoon was a miniature of our married life—full of surprises and challenges, pleasurable but unpredictable, eventful and providential.

Lessons From Landmines

Married life is not a bed of roses. I once heard the story of a bride who as soon as she entered the home sat in the rocking chair singing, "When all my labors and trials are o'er." Newlyweds face dangerous landmines like roles, sex, money, in-laws, and incompatibility, and small ones like their own idiosyncrasies. And when we wear the shoes of selfishness, these mines can blow the relationship to pieces and bring the marriage to ruin! No wonder the divorce rate stands at 50 percent in America, and it is not much better in some other areas. That is why premarital counseling is crucial.

We were back in Georgetown eager and ready to set up our home in the lovely two-bedroom house that was spacious enough for us. However, we were totally unprepared for what happened soon after crossing the threshold. That first week we stepped on about five landmines! But from each experience, we learned a valuable lesson.

Our first landmine was our living room suite. When we went looking for furniture we had seen two sets that were possibilities, but we did not discuss which of the two sets we would purchase. We could not get the apartment before the wedding, so I thought we would make the final selection and purchase the set after the honeymoon. Gordon on the other hand, wanted to have everything ready before we returned so he went ahead and purchased the set I did not specifically like, had it delivered, and someone set it up while we were away without telling me. I guess he wanted to surprise me. His apparently good gesture caused grave discontent. It was a real case of an old Guyanese saying, "Good you do, bad you see." Unfortunately, this impasse lasted several days because I could not bring myself to talk about the problem. After I had sulked several days, I finally settled down to accepting it and moved on.

Our first lesson was: Communicate! Learn to communicate! It is the lifeblood of a lasting relationship. Share what bothers you, tell how you feel, say what you want, discuss it, pray about it, and move on.

Communicate! Learn to communicate! It is the lifeblood of a lasting relationship. Share what bothers you, tell how you feel, say what you want, discuss it, pray about it, and move on.

We were simply delighted to open the many wedding gifts we received, and make note of the household items we needed to purchase. As we untied the packages, Gordon made mention of pricing the gifts and paying a tithe on them. I was mad at the idea! I had never heard of such a thing and opposed it. This was another landmine! However, I calmed down when he pointed out that the tithe was just one tenth of what the total cost would have been if we had to purchase all those items. Over the years we have adopted that principle. Come to think about it, Abraham paid tithes to Melchizedek from the spoils of war (Gen. 14:18–20). Beyond that, we decided to return twenty percent of our income—ten percent tithe, ten percent offering. And indeed we have experienced the fulfillment of God's promise. He said, "If I will not open for you the windows of heaven and pour out for you such a blessing that there will not be room enough to receive it" (Mal. 3:10).

So we learned a second lesson: Be faithful in returning tithe to God. He always keeps His promises.

I have always heard the experienced say, "Don't fool yourself that you can change your mate." And I found that to be true. After showering, I liked then, and still do now, to freshen up with some powder and perfume. But Gordon did not. So I talked to him about it, and even bought some mild scents for men. But it was all to no avail. So I gave up in despair. I was experiencing a third landmine! Years later, when I had forgotten all about it, Gordon worked in an office where he observed that one of his male counterparts whom he admired left a captivating scent when he passed by. Guess what? My dear husband got out the unused bottles of cologne, and he continues to use scents up to this day!

So here was a third lesson: Don't sweat the small stuff! An African proverb says, "Before you get married, keep both eyes open; and after you marry, close one eye!"

An African proverb says, "Before you get married, keep both eyes open; and after you marry, close one eye!"

Our fourth landmine was money. And it was a big one! When it was time to put our two incomes on the table, Gordon had none! As a bachelor he had neither the time nor the desire to manage his money. He said that he would often keep his salary in his pocket and pay bills as needed. And when the money was gone, he was done! I became very upset and told him so in no uncertain tones. When, as time went by, he realized that I was the better financier, he willingly left me to take care of the money, which I do to this day.

We learned a fourth vital lesson: It's not "my money, nor your money, but our money." Let the one better in money matters manage the incomes.

Finally, there was a landmine called pride. As I look back on those early days of marriage, I deeply regret my pride, and I am glad that my husband forgave me many times. By the way, when you talk about pride, I was the epitome of it. Would you believe that I was so proud that if someone brushed against me on the road, I would wipe it off? One day a lady in downtown Water Street saw my reaction and rebuked me by saying, "If you don't want anyone to touch you, stay at home or make your own street!" That surely gave me something to think about!

When things went wrong, Gordon was always willing to say those most difficult words, "I am sorry. Please forgive me." Even though

I sometimes recognized that I was wrong, I could not bring myself to admit my fault. And after we talked things over, we would pray and move on. God indeed kept us while we navigated those dangerous landmines.

Lesson five was: Don't be too proud to say, "I was wrong. I am sorry." And learn to forgive. Remember this: "The difference between 'United' and 'Untied' is where you put the 'I'." Don't let self get in the way of marital happiness.

Yes, in those early years of marriage we had many challenging experiences. But regardless of what came our way, we were committed to each other and determined to make our marriage work. We remembered that it was God who brought our lives together. After fifty-two years of married life, I think of marriage in phases.

- The wedding—commitment to love—to have and to hold, to love and be loved

- The honeymoon—consummation of love—sexual intimacy, to know and be known

- The marriage—confirmation of love—disagreements and trials—in love forever, "till death do us part"

Chapter 11

Our First District

West Berbice, Here We Come!

After returning from our honeymoon, we lived for a while in Georgetown while I continued teaching at the school and Gordon traveled back and forth to his churches in West Berbice. Then the president had the brilliant idea that we should go to Paraima to head the work of the so-called Davis Indian Mission that served the Amerindians. Gordon would be superintendent and pastor, and I would be the school principal. Gordon did not mind going, and I was thrilled at the idea because I had my sights on higher education in America and that would facilitate saving. However, the item was discussed at the committee meeting, and we were told that one member asked, "Why send two valuable workers to the interior when there is such a great need for them here?" Finally, they decided not to upset the apple cart and just leave us where we were. I'm sure my mom was happy at the decision because she had expressed some fears.

So we packed and moved from the residential Queenstown in the city to No. 30 Village, West Coast Berbice. A church member with a thriving copra (coconut dried in the sun) business put in a water pump to siphon the water to the upper level. He also got us electricity from 6:00 p.m. to 9:00 p.m. It was spacious, very comfortable, and had natural air conditioning—God's refreshing sea breeze. I liked it.

Since I was still school principal, this move meant that I had to travel three hours by train on weekends. On Friday afternoons I would

Chapter 11 Our First District

purchase a first class ticket, choose a cubicle on board the train, and ride comfortably to No. 30, then do the return trip on Sundays back to my parents' home in the city. When the country was racially divided, wisdom dictated that I forego the first class, and choose a carriage that had people of the other race in it, since attacks were made on trains, busses, and other types of transportation. This made traveling a challenge.

Lessons in Humility

We lived at No. 30 Village for two years, and during that time God humbled my pride. No more did I travel in the cubicle in first class on the train. No more did I have the luxury of a car, for all that my pastor husband had to manage six churches was a bicycle! No more paved roads! You see, the main roadway in West Berbice was made of burnt earth, which was dusty in dry weather and muddy in wet weather. No more dressing for church with fancy expensive clothes because the parishioners were simple country folk. No more comfort, for at times I had to ride the one overcrowded public bus when we had to visit the other churches in the district. And I was pushed and squeezed by the "common folk" who could care less about me or my nice clothes and smooth skin.

But I took it all in stride because God was remaking me while trying to lead me. I can join the blind hymn writer Fanny J. Crosby in singing,

> All the way my Savior leads me;
> What have I to ask beside?
> Can I doubt His tender mercy,
> Who through life has been my Guide?
> Heav'nly peace, divinest comfort,
> Here by faith in Him to dwell

For I know, whate'er befall me,
Jesus doeth all things well.
("All the Way My Savior Leads Me," 1875)

And by the way, through the decades, that has also been Gordon's favorite hymn.

We decided to delay having children because the goal was to continue our education in the United States. But some of the dear "nosy sisters" of the church thought I was having a problem conceiving. One of them in particular, whom we called Dear Aunt, always brought me eggs, fruit, vegetables, and any other produce of her land. Among the fruits was one that Guyanese called "downes." So whenever she came, she would say, "Sister Waveney, I have brought you some 'breeding' downes. And I'll bring you some more later on." Of course, I would just smile at her.

It is interesting how God works. Sometimes when things go "wrong" for us, it is just part of His plan. That was our situation with the poor car purchase we made. As a result, we had to cancel the idea of immediate study in America and decided on raising a family.

Even though I was in the district only on weekends, I was very active in the church. I was Sabbath School superintendent at No. 30/Union Church, and I also worked with the children and youth. I marvel at how God used my little knowledge of piano playing to practice a youth quartet to sing "Going Afar." We met on Friday nights, and on the little organ of the church, we practiced one part at a time. Then the time came for them to make their debut. That Sabbath morning the church organist did the honor of accompanying them, and when they were finished, the church came alive with a resounding "Amen!" This response encouraged the quartet so that they continued the

Friday night practices, and that blossomed into a concert that packed the little community hall to capacity. The main feature of the concert was the dramatization of the story of Noah and the flood. It was a joy to work with the youth of the Union Church. Indeed, little becomes much as we place it in the Master's hand. Remember the little boy's lunch of five loaves and two fishes? It fed 5,000 men besides women and children (Matt. 14:13–21).

Historic Belladrum Campaign

As pastor of six churches and two companies many miles apart from each other, and equipped with only a bicycle, Gordon did not always sleep in our home at Union during the week I was away. In fact, he had five other "homes"—one in each village that hosted a church. And he was introduced to these residences by his predecessor, Pastor Fred Morales. These faithful saints shared their facilities and meals with any visiting pastor! I remember the house of the elderly couple at the turn of the road in Mahaica, and the lovely house of Brother and Sister Charles in Mahaicony. Then there was another elderly sister in Rosignol who lived near the ferry, and at Ithaca it was the home of the Andersons whose brilliant children have achieved academic and professional success. I visited and slept in almost all of those homes.

However, the smallest place, a ramshackle of a house screaming for repair, was the home of Brother and Sister Ross at Belladrum. But if the elder's home was challenging, the church home was appalling! Its roof was made of palm leaves, its posts were wooden rods, and its walls were made of straw plastered with mud! It stood in stark contrast with the fine Anglican Church that was considered the village church. The Lord enabled Gordon to inspire the members to tear down that eyesore and construct a beautiful new building on land donated by the Ross family. Soon the building was dedicated, which reminded me of the dedication of Solomon's temple (1 Kings 8).

Immediately after the dedication, Gordon conducted the "Belladrum for Christ" Campaign, and Mission President Milton Neblett assigned Pastor S. Wailu and Pastor Philbert Ramotar to work in the program. Just about that time, there was a problem at the Anglican Church that caused some of its members to grow dissatisfied, which opened their hearts to attend the Adventist meetings. The villagers packed the tent each night, and at the end of the series, seventy-five persons accepted Jesus and the doctrines of the church and were baptized! The big question was: Where could we baptize so many people? The always-resourceful President Neblett had an answer. He ordered a large inflatable swimming pool from the United States. And what a sensation it was! Such a large number of persons baptized in a country village was historic for Guyanese. And when those baptized from other churches in the district through campaigns conducted by laypersons were added, the district had more than one hundred baptisms that year!

With such a large increase in its membership, the church faced a new problem: the new church building was now too small! So they added two wings to the structure. Belladrum had now replaced Union as the largest church in the district! At present, the Belladrum Church is still the leader. It has a large new concrete building with a seating capacity of 500 thanks to the investment of Drs. Leon and Colwick Wilson, whose mother was baptized in the "Belladrum for Christ" Campaign! Today these brothers support the ministry of Happy Family Bible Seminars. In fact, Leon is our ministry's largest annual donor, and he

Chapter 11 Our First District

also serves on our board of directors. Thanks, Leon, for your generosity.

During the Belladrum campaign, the mission looked with favor on authorizing a car for Gordon. We found one from a dealer who was also my brother's mechanic. We were attracted to a special feature—the front seat could be lowered to a lying position. This would be good for either of us to sleep while we traveled from church to church. And the price was right! It cost about US $1,000.00, although that was a lot of money at the time. Unfortunately, the car was a lemon. Driving around in the city was good, but when we drove long distances in the country, it was a nightmare! The engine would cut off frequently, and we had to push it to get started again. We took it to the local mechanic who offered to buy it for about half the cost, but we did not accept the offer. Eventually, we had to write it off as our loss. So there we were again riding the bus, or the train, or whatever we could. That is why we decided to have children instead of pursuing an education.

Since our loving Lord had blessed the Belladrum campaign so significantly, Gordon set his sight on conducting two campaigns simultaneously—one at Mahaicony and the other at Ithaca miles apart from each other. He planned to start the Mahaicony one at 5:00 p.m., and then travel to Ithaca for a later night meeting. Pastor Neblett shared his concern, but Gordon did not listen. He was young, strong, and zealous for the work. He now admits that it was a crazy thing to do! We were all relieved when the plan was aborted because of racial unrest in Mahaicony. Then "tragedy" struck!

Chapter 12

Why, Lord? Why?

Gordon was and still is an excellent preacher, teacher, and evangelist. He is an organized, diligent, hard working, and God-fearing pastor who still knows how to wrestle with God in prayer. When I asked him how he knew he wanted to be a minister, he said that he did not have a dramatic call like Saul on the Damascus road, or like Martin Luther struck down by lightning. He likened it to the call of Samuel. Since he was a child, he knew that he wanted to be a pastor. It was a daily growing experience like the boy Samuel who grew up and ministered in the temple. As a boy, Gordon loved to read the Bible. He studied both the junior and senior courses of the Voice of Prophecy and just simply loved to work in the "temple."

So what happened next ushered in a time of wavering faith and much questioning.

Dashed Expectations at Ithaca

The abortion of the Mahaicony campaign allowed him to focus on the Ithaca campaign. I could not attend every night because there was limited housing for both of us over such a lengthy period of time. This meant that I had to stay home alone. But that was soon to change.

Around midnight one night I was awakened by Sister Benjamin knocking and calling me. She declared that the Indians were coming! The tension between the two races was still raging. After I got dressed, I started to gather some belongings. Then I remembered that I had the

Chapter 12 Why, Lord? Why?

church's money, which I could not carry because of the weighty coins.. I was the acting treasurer while the treasurer was recuperating from an illness. I then decided that since I could not take the Lord's money I could not take mine either! Instead, I picked up my Bible and prayerfully waited for the command from the men guarding the homes. Thank God the Indians never came. That compelled the members of Ithaca to fix up one of the rooms in the Andersons' unfinished house so we could be there together until the campaign was over. That was pleasing to me, and so I packed my suitcase and was ready for the long stay there. But that stay was to end prematurely.

Around midnight one night I was awakened by Sister Benjamin knocking and calling me. She declared that the Indians were coming!

It was an unforgettable scene! The small church was packed to capacity! It was standing room only on the inside, with people on the steps and around the building by the open windows. We could hear the annoying buzz and feel the stings of scores of pesky mosquitoes. In full view was the smoke arising from a coal pot, a small portable furnace positioned near the pulpit to ward off the pests. The air was charged with high expectation that something good was about to happen. The sermon that night dealt with the fascinating topic on law and grace. Without a microphone, Gordon preached with power using effective homemade visual aids on cardboard. And in spite of the distractions, the people listened intently. The Spirit of God was surely in that place that night. Like the Belladrum campaign, this Ithaca one was sure to result in another landslide victory for God!

But the next morning Gordon could not speak! He could only whisper, and he did so with much pain. As the day wore on, it was evident that there would be no meeting that night. Nor would there be a meeting any other night! Much to the dismay of the members of that small church by the side of the road in Ithaca, the campaign had to be terminated. And the big question on my mind, and on the minds of so many others was, "God, why? Why did You allow that to happen?"

Seeing the Silver Lining

Since we had to repay the car loan and our hope of further education was put on hold, we decided to start our family. In fact, our first child, Esther, was conceived during that Ithaca campaign! Now the dear "nosy" sisters were singing a different song! They referred to Gordon as doubting Zacharias and predicted that at the birth of the special "boy child" he would regain his voice. Would their prediction come true?

The ear, nose, and throat specialist in Georgetown gave some medication and instructed that Gordon rest his voice completely for one month. But month after month went by, and there was no improvement. During this time, we relocated to the city and stayed at the home of my parents. That was convenient for me since I was still principal of the school and now pregnant with our first child. Like Zacharias, Gordon's way of communicating was by writing. He used piles and piles of notebooks. It was a very trying time for both of us. O God, what next? was our constant question.

But God knew what He was doing. He always does! It was during this time that Gordon and I started studying the Bible deeply together. One of the books we examined together was Judges. He showed me how to search for text explanation by reading the Bible Commentary and how to get further insights from the inspired writings of Ellen G. White. Another book we studied together was Philippians. For me, the Bible came so alive that I simply enjoyed studying it more and more. And still do!

God was saying, "I still love you, My child." He had a plan that at the time our myopic vision did not allow us to see. And it was not easy to heed Peter's council, "Beloved, do not think it strange concerning the fiery trial which is to try you, as though some strange thing happened to you; but rejoice ... that when His glory is revealed, you also may be glad with exceeding joy" (1 Peter 4:12, 13). How could one rejoice amid such uncertainty? By learning to trust Him! As the sayings go, "Trust Him where we cannot trace Him," and "Trust His heart when you cannot see His hand."

Since Gordon could not speak, the innovative Mission President Neblett had another bright idea! He had Gordon appointed as director of the Lay Activities (now Personal Ministries) Department. He was impressed with how the lay preachers in West Berbice performed and wanted to see that enthusiasm countrywide. So he imported a portable battery-powered desktop microphone, the size of a small suitcase, for Gordon's use.

As Gordon threw all his energies into lay evangelism, the Lord empowered him to inspire hundreds of lay preachers, male and female, to participate in a program called "Thousand Drive in Sixty Five." Armed with a new book of sermons, and empowered by the Spirit, these laypersons were motivated to baptize 1,000 souls in 1965. The president was enthused, and personally accompanied Gordon church by church, district by district throughout the mission. The plan was to have a massive baptism of the candidates at the mission's first camp meeting in conjunction with the mission session that year. God blessed the program richly, and over 800 souls were baptized. "To God be the glory!" It was at that convocation that both Gordon and Roy, his brother-in-law, were ordained to the gospel ministry.

The conference session that followed soon after was marked by high drama! The ever-innovative mission president wanted to showcase Adventism to the whole country. So he paid for a four-page insert in one of the leading daily newspapers. And he singlehandedly wrote all the articles! These included the massive welfare and food-feeding program, the medical work being done by Davis Memorial Hospital, the constituency meetings, and much more. Knowing whom he was going to recommend as his choice for departmental directors, he included that report also. But then he had to give the insert to the newspaper long beforehand, so he instructed that they wait for his directive as to the day to publish the article.

Unfortunately, the newspaper did not wait! So before the nominating committee could finish its work, the newspaper had published the "results!" And pandemonium broke out! No one talked about the evangelistic and public relations benefits of a full-page insert showcasing the Adventist Church to the whole country. All they saw was a president who was manipulating the process. He was accused of favoritism and of bypassing the senior men for his favorite junior pastors. Two names on his list were Gordon Martinborough for lay activities (now personal ministries), and Roy McGarrell for education. So the nominating committee retaliated by refusing to accept all of them. Maybe because of the success of the

Chapter 12 Why, Lord? Why?

"Thousand Drive" program, they kept Martinborough, but they did not elect McGarrell.

The pastors, lay leaders, and people were divided: some for the president and others against him. People had sit-in sessions at the mission compound, and teachers with their students from the Adventist high school picketed the office. The Caribbean Union sent a commission of enquiry, and as a result, the energetic, visionary president had to leave Guyana.

It's a Girl—Esther!

It was while Gordon was traveling on one of his motivational trips to West Coast Demerara that Esther was born. That Sabbath morning I went to church as usual, taught children's class as usual, returned home and had lunch as usual with the rest of the family. After washing the dishes, I went for a siesta. And as soon as I lay down my water broke. Completely ignorant of what was going on, I called Magnel who had just returned from nursing school in England with both nursing and midwifery experience. She calmly explained what had happened and told me to prepare to go to the hospital.

I could sense the anxiety in Mom's voice as we arrived and were told there were no beds available. The small but very popular Davis Memorial Hospital was full. And there was a patient lying on a gurney, and another one waiting on the operating room table. There simply was "no room at the inn!" That was about 4:00 p.m. So I had to sit and wait for an opening. Fortunately, my sister was with me instructing me to breathe deeply during the pain and updating the nurse in charge on the length of time between contractions. Just about the time when the contractions were coming fast and unbearable, the doctor arrived and discharged a patient. At about 8:00 p.m. I was placed on the gurney and soon went into the delivery room. And at 8:24 p.m. baby Esther loudly announced her arrival!

Would you believe that I knew without ultrasound that I was going to have a girl? Would you believe that I had a dream that my sister would be the one to take care of me? That night I slept on the operating table, waiting patiently to see my baby girl. I did not see her until the next day, and during that time I wondered if there was a problem. But elsewhere the dear little one was screaming her little lungs out trying to adjust to her new environment outside of the womb while the nurses were complaining. How different it is today! The newborn is immediately put in the arms of the smiling mother. And that's a good thing for both mother and child!

The dear sisters of West Coast Berbice were false prophetesses! They had given two false prophecies! The baby was not a boy; it was a girl! And Gordon still could not speak audibly without his portable device! I continued teaching, and we lived in a house on the mission compound.

After the "Thousand Drive" initiative, attention was turned to the "Big Week" program! This was one of the dreaded activities where each church was assigned a quota of missionary books for members to sell. Year after year unsold books were returned and stockpiled at the mission office! But 1965 was different. The Lord inspired Gordon to reframe the program as "October Ten Thousand." The goal was to sell 10,000 copies of the book of the year. Church after church was visited with its quota of books, and each member was given a canvass to memorize. The result was astounding! The people rallied to the challenge, and the books moved from office to church to community and did not return to storage! "To God be the glory!" By this time Gordon's voice had improved slightly, but he still depended on his small portable microphone.

Then the Boy—Samuel!

I was now pregnant with our second child, and because Esther was still a baby, I asked to be relieved of my role as principal of the growing elementary school. However, one day at a staff meeting my successor told the teachers that I was relieved of my leadership role because the mission was not pleased with my work. I was shocked! In my anger, I vehemently responded to this untruth. This staff meeting became very stormy as other teachers joined in expressing their own dislikes. We participated in this tirade and did not care whether the children were listening or playing.

News of the incident reached the conference office before I arrived to pick up Gordon, and I was confronted by one of the saintly workers there. I realized my mistake and felt terribly ashamed at my outburst. So, before settling in for the night, I asked God to forgive me. In my private devotion the next morning, I read a statement from the pen of Ellen G. White that drove me to tears. I wept bitterly as I realized that my action could have impacted some teacher or some child negatively. And more than that, I had crucified Jesus afresh! So during assembly that morning, I publicly apologized to her and to the children. A few months after that incident, I made a visit to the mission office to see the director who was the source of the misinformation. Even though I addressed the matter in much calmer tones, it caused me great stress, and the result could have been catastrophic.

Early the next morning I started having birth pains that sent me to the hospital, and I almost lost our second child. Dr. Harold Gates immediately ordered medication that made me sleep the entire day. I left the hospital the next morning feeling as "fit as a fiddle" physically, emotionally, and spiritually. On a Sabbath morning four months later, Sammy was getting ready to enter the world. And once again Magnel was with me. She was then a staff nurse at the hospital and was working the evening shift. She stayed home with me during the morning, and I accompanied her to work that evening. And again there were no beds! Since the birth signs were not acute, I returned home after her shift that Saturday night.

About five o'clock Sunday morning an unbearable pain indicated that the time was now right. I went to the hospital and was taken to the delivery room right away. Around 7:00 a.m. Sammy was born. And once again Gordon was not there to witness his child's birth because, just like Esther, Sammy had arrived before the scheduled date. This time Gordon was much farther away! He was at Linden, the bauxite mining town sixty-five miles up the Demerara River. And in those days, the town was only accessible by boat. I could hear the joy and anxiety in Gordon's voice when I told him by phone that he had a baby boy. And again I knew the child's gender in advance, because I had seen it in a dream.

Soon after Sammy was born, we were on the move again. This time it was a lovely split-level duplex in residential Laluni Street, Queenstown. Gordon still worked at the office, I was still teaching, and now we owned a good car—a white Volkswagen. We were very comfortable. The beauty and quiet of our home was matched by the peace and quiet at the mission. There was now an interim president, and a white American, Steve Willsey, served as secretary-treasurer. When he knew of Gordon's voice problem, Steve suggested that he should leave the country for help. Contact was made with a specialist in Puerto Rico and travel arrangements were made. All hopes ran high!

Chapter 13

He Really Loves Me!

Drama at Laluni Street

One afternoon Gordon called to say that he was bringing home a young man from New Amsterdam who had come to the city to look for work but had no place to stay. We took him in and treated him like a son. Did not the apostle Paul say that we ought to entertain strangers because some have entertained angels in unawares (Heb. 13:2)?

Shirley and her two children, Andre and Fern, also came to stay with us because Roy had gone to Trinidad to work in the massive Cleveland campaign in Port of Spain. This evangelistic series became historic because it resulted in the largest number of baptisms from a single campaign up to that time. Over 700 persons were baptized! And a follow-up program conducted by Pastor George Rainey brought the total to over 1,000 baptisms and the birth of Cleveland Temple Church.

Soon Gordon received his travel documents and headed to Puerto Rico, leaving two women, each with two small children, along with the young man and two cars in the carport. We had a helper during the day, and when she left, I took care of the four children. After spending two weeks in Puerto Rico, Gordon returned with the diagnosis that brought hope to our hearts. The specialist said that it was a sinus drain that was causing the voice problem, and he prescribed some medication. Unfortunately, the tablets did not help. The diagnosis was not accurate.

While the men were away, Shirley decided to learn to drive the family car. When the instructor came, the children went with her. One Sunday afternoon the young man also went with them. About midnight the same night, I was awakened by a loud banging on the door. It was the police. He asked how many cars we had in the carport, and when we looked, to our surprise we saw only one! We were still in shock when another police officer arrived with the young man. Although he did not know how to drive, nor did he own a license, that restless youth got little Andre to give him the car keys. Then he snuck out in the night, pushed the car into the street, drove it to the city, and crashed it at a roundabout. When Roy returned, he got it repaired. Sadly we had to let the young man go his way.

While at Laluni Street, there was more drama. My three-year-old niece Denise came to spend a day with us. Somehow she spotted the bottle of pills, and thinking that the tablets were candy, she swallowed some of them. No one knows how many she took! As soon as I got home for lunch, our helper broke the news, and we rushed her to the hospital. Thank God she suffered no ill effect from the incident. We learned a quick lesson to keep drugs out of the reach of children.

More Drama!

The new mission president, Pastor Lionel Arthur, wanted to downsize the number of departmental directors at the office, and since the atmosphere after the stormy mission session was still unpleasant, Gordon volunteered to leave and serve as pastor for the West Demerara district, which had six churches. So we left our lovely Laluni home to look for one across the river. Strangely enough, in all of the moves I neither grumbled nor complained. We found a relatively decent two-bedroom house at Crane, a village about a mile from the Demerara River, which separated the city from the West Coast. The only means of transportation from this village to the city was by a steamer that plied the river at scheduled times of the day and nothing at night. This location made it convenient for me, who was still teaching in Georgetown, and Sister Solomon, our faithful home helper, to commute between the city and the coast. Gordon would take me to the ferry in the morning and transport her to our home, and do the reverse in the afternoon.

One morning we were going down the stairs on our way to the ferry when Gordon tripped and two-year-old Sammy went flying out of his hands and landed on the concrete below.

One morning we were going down the stairs on our way to the ferry when Gordon tripped and two-year-old Sammy went flying out of his hands and landed on the concrete below. This knocked Sammy unconscious! Trembling with fear, I picked up the lifeless form, rushed him upstairs, put his head under flowing water with the hope that this would revive him. But it did not! There was neither doctor nor hospital nearby, so we had to wait on the ferry to take him to the city. The trip seemed to take hours! We were grateful to God when the doctor finally told us that he had a concussion but would be alright. He slept that whole day in the hospital, and when we went to get him, we found him playing with the other children in the room. Thank God he was alive and well! (So,

Chapter 13 He Really Loves Me!

Sam, He saved your life twice—in utero and in infancy. Make sure He saves you eternally.)

Soon a third child was on its way. But the stress and strain of the daily commute during the week and the travel to the various churches on Sabbath from early morning to late night with two-year-old Esther and one-year-old Samuel took its toll on me, and I had a miscarriage. I was later told by my nurse-midwife sisters that the attendant nurse who took care of me across the river did some things that could have led to infection and possible death. That was scary to hear, but by God's grace, I suffered no ill effects.

My First Sermon

It was in this West Demerara district that we really began working as a team in ministry. Ingathering time had arrived. This was the time that church members solicited donations from people in the community to aid the medical, educational, and welfare programs of the church. But Gordon still had limited use of his voice. So as we traveled from church to church, he presented the strategy for reaching the goal, and I preached the sermon. This was my first time behind the pulpit as a preacher! My first sermon was titled "Up, for this is the day!" It was taken from the book of Judges, which we had studied together.

The Spirit of God was at work, and the members rallied to the challenge. I also did my own solicitation in my neighborhood, and the results were astounding! The district goal was reached in the first week, the super goal in the second week, and by the third week the district had tripled its basic goal! In every church we lifted our voices and sang the song of victory "To God be the Glory" long before the mission's closing date. Throughout the district we witnessed the reality of Judges 5:2: "When leaders lead … when the people willingly offer themselves." The people had a mind to work, not only in harvesting dollars but also in harvesting souls for God's kingdom.

Work in the district was expanding. I left the Georgetown school, and we started a school at Anna Catherina with about a dozen students in three grades. Compton Gaskin, a young God-fearing and focused youth, was employed as my assistant. After a year or so our enrollment grew, and Colin Parkinson joined the staff. Not long after that a ministerial intern arrived. Young Hilton Garnett had graduated from CUC and was assigned to our district. From the airport he went to the mission office, and from there he arrived at our home, where he stayed for a few months. Pastor Garnett later became one of the most beloved pastors, and he eventually became one of the most outstanding presidents of the Guyana Conference. When he talks about his work experience, he jokingly says, "From the airport, to the office, to the district, and into the Martinboroughs' home."

Fear of Being Lost!

Not long after my miscarriage, something went terribly wrong. I suffered from a deadly fear. I often felt I was going to die. I had episodes of tachycardia where my heart would feel like a race car! I visited the doctor often, but the tests to find the possible cause always came back negative. Many nights I had little or no sleep. In fact, I was afraid to fall asleep. The physician gave me valium, but still my eyes were sunken from lack of sleep. Fear gripped my every move. Many times I thought I was going to have a heart attack and die from the loud beatings of my heart. Often my mind played tricks on me. I could hear a voice in my head saying, "You better not go here or there, for if you do you will not return home alive."

Since the cause was not physical, it could have been psychological, but there were no psychiatrists available in those days. In retrospect I think the underlying reason was spiritual. I was uncertain of my salvation. I read the Bible and prayed earnestly, but I did not understand that salvation was by faith in Jesus, and not by keeping the law. For example, on Sabbath mornings I would vow within my mind that I would keep the Sabbath holy and not think my own thoughts. But shortly after secular thoughts about things I needed to buy would come rushing into my mind! I was in the same dilemma as the disciples who cried, "Who then can be saved?" (Matt. 19:25). I did not realize that I was trying to be obedient in my own strength.

The greatest dread of all was my fear of God. I knew that Jesus loved me, but I did not know that God the Father loved me. Of course, I taught the children at home and at school the favorite song, "Jesus loves me this I know." But did God the Father love me? Stories like His refusal of Cain's offering, God's slaying of Uzzah for trying to prevent the ark from falling, and His rejection of King Saul filled my soul with fear. As such, I was sure that I had committed the unpardonable sin, and like King Saul, I would be lost. This fear and loss of sleep caused me to lose weight, and I was reduced to ninety-two pounds!

There were a few times when the sunshine of hope seemed to pierce through the darkness of despair. One of them was when Esther, who was then two or three, prayed for me. That morning I was lying in bed not preparing for school, disgusted and discouraged, when she came to my bedside and said a prayer for me. I don't recall what she said, but the effect was instant! I immediately got out of bed and got ready for school. Another was when my assistant Compton, a very spiritual young man, told me, "It's not feelings, but faith," and he also prayed for me. And yet another was when someone sang a special song, which said,

> The tempter to my soul has said,
>
> "There's no help in God for thee;"
>
> Lord! lift Thou up Thy servant's head;
>
> My glory, shield, and solace be.
>
> Thus to the Lord I raised my cry;
>
> He heard me from His holy hill;
>
> At His command the waves rolled by;
>
> He beckoned, and the winds were still.
>
> I will not fear, though armed throngs
>
> Surround my steps in all their wrath;
>
> Salvation to the Lord belongs;
>
> His presence guards His people's path.
>
> (James Montgomery, 1882)

Unfortunately the effect was only temporary. Soon the shadows reappeared and blotted out the golden rays of sunshine.

God Is Love!

We lived in Crane for about a year when the owners told us they needed their house. While looking for a replacement, we lived with God-fearing Sister Ada Miller at Anna Catherina. When we lodged there, she told us stories of demonic confrontations that confirmed my belief in a real devil and a real God. One of the most amazing stories was the attempt by the devil to destroy the Bible. I don't remember the details except the fact that regardless of

Chapter 13 He Really Loves Me!

several attempts to burn the Bible, it just did not succumb to the flames.

One night I had a dream in which I saw myself walking as it were inside of Jesus. His big body covered my small frame. In the morning I awoke and wrote a poem, which unfortunately was lost amid our many moves. However, the first two lines were, "Like Abraham, Lord, I want to be; Faithful, obedient, trusting Thee." I didn't realize the significance of the dream until years later when I read the text, "I will greatly rejoice in the Lord, my soul shall be joyful in my God; for He has clothed me with the garments of salvation, He has covered me with the robe of righteousness" (Isa. 61:10).

The concept of "being covered" is beautifully portrayed when the Father covered His prodigal son with His robe to hide the filth of the pigpen (Luke 15:11–32). One hymn writer puts it this way,

> Look upon Jesus, sinless is He;
>
> Father, impute His life unto me.
>
> My life of scarlet, my sin and woe,
>
> Covered with His life, whiter than snow.
>
> (F. E. Belden, "Cover With His Life," 1899)

But in spite of this assurance, I still suffered the fear of being lost. When a slight earthquake tremor rattled the small house, I made a dash for the door! Days turned into months and months into a new year, and I was still troubled.

Then one morning I was reading John 20, which tells of the encounter of Mary Magdalene with Jesus in the garden on resurrection morning. After Jesus revealed Himself to her, He said, "Do not cling to Me, for I have not yet ascended to My Father; but go to My brethren and say to them, 'I am ascending *to My Father and your Father*, and *to My God and your God*'" (John 20:17, italics supplied). Suddenly, I experienced a breakthrough! It was as if a light bulb lit up in my head as I began to reflect on the words, "My Father and your Father, your God and my God." God was *my* Father!

I thought about my own father who loved and cared for not just one, but nine of us, his children! I remembered how he worked to provide food, clothing, and shelter. I mused about how he listened to us and gave us what we asked him for, and much more! Then I began to realize that if God is my Father He loves me too. This fact was later confirmed by what Pastor Morris Venden said in a sermon at the La Sierra Church that God loves us and it is the devil who wants us to believe otherwise. That day I could have jumped to the ceiling and screamed "God the Father loves me!"

"Satan pictured the Creator as a being who is watching with jealous eye to discern the errors and mistakes of men, that He may visit judgments upon them. It was to remove this dark shadow ... that Jesus came to live among men."

Subsequently I read in the small Ellen White classic, *Steps to Christ*, "'God is love' is written upon every opening bud, upon every spire of springing grass.... Satan led men to conceive of God as a being whose chief attribute is stern justice,—one who is a severe judge, a harsh, exacting creditor. He pictured the Creator as a being who is watching with jealous eye to discern the errors and mistakes of men, that He may visit judgments upon them. It was to remove this dark shadow ... that Jesus came to live among men" (pp. 10, 11).

Catch the imagery as F. L. Lehman tries to paint a picture of the fathomless love of God in the hymn "The Love of God": "The love of God is greater far than tongue or pen can ever tell; it goes beyond the highest star, and reaches to the lowest hell.... Could we with ink the ocean fill, and were the sky of parchment made; Were every stalk on earth a quill [pen], and every man a scribe by trade; To write the love of God above, would drain the ocean dry; Nor could the scroll contain the whole, though spread from side to side."

You could imagine my joy knew no bounds! In my soul I was jumping to the ceiling! And straightway I began telling others the good news of God's love. It was the start of a new era of my life. I had experienced the love of God in Jesus, and joy and peace now flooded my soul.

I was experiencing a new life in Christ! It echoed the theme song "New Life" by John Peterson that Gordon used on his *New Life* radio program, on which I spoke a few times.

It was indeed the dawn of a new day—a bright and glorious morning for me. "Thanks be to God for His indescribable gift" (2 Cor. 9:15).

Part Three:

First Stay in the United States

Chapter 14

Arrival in America

Since the Puerto Rico effort to attend to Gordon's voice had failed, Steve Willsey, the determined secretary-treasurer, turned his efforts to America. Then came the day when we were told that the mission had arranged for him to go to Loma Linda University Medical Center. As such we sold our belongings and moved in with my parents in their Belvoir Court suburban home. Soon after Gordon was on his way to California. Strangely enough, our early dream was to go to America to study. Now we were going at a different time and for a different reason. This reminds me of the story of Lazarus. Jesus did not show up when they felt that He should. But when they thought He was late, He was right on time!

While we were awaiting word from Gordon, I made a strange request from God. I asked Him to show myself as He sees me. I remember telling Mom and Dad one morning after worship what I had prayed for and that the answer I received was that I was selfish. And so I began praying that God would help me to put others before myself, remembering that the acronym of *joy* is **J**esus first, **O**thers next, **Y**ourself last. Someone said, "It is the love of self that destroys our peace." And Ellen White declared that, "There can be no growth or fruitfulness in the life that is centered in self" (*Christ's Object lessons*, p. 67).

Vocal Chords Damaged!

After two to three weeks of much praying and patient waiting, a letter finally arrived. Anxiously I tore open the envelope and read that tests revealed that the vocal chords were damaged from wrong use of the voice. Pastors in Guyana in those days did not have the luxury of any sound system and had to project their voice as best as they could. Then I read the good news! The vocal chords could be corrected with rest and therapy. This would require time. Thank You Jesus! Gordon would be able to speak again! He would be able to preach without discomfort!' We lifted our voice in praise to our heavenly Father.

With Gordon needing therapy, the children and I prepared to join him in California. The day came when we were to depart. With suitcases packed and tickets in hand, we said our fond farewells to Mom and Papa Marts at the airport, and three-year-old Esther and two-year-old Sammy and I boarded a KLM flight bound for the United States. After making a few stops on the way and spending hours in the sky, we finally saw the lights of America and landed at the busy Los Angeles airport. Wow! We had reached the "promised land" at last! At least that was the idea many had about America. Gordon and Pastor Neblett were waiting for us. Soon we were on our way to begin a new life, to record another chapter of God's faithfulness, and experience more of His miracles.

Milton to the Rescue!

Gordon was staying with George Williams, a fellow Guyanese studying medicine at Loma Linda University, and his wife, Shirley. So there is where we went. We lived with them for about a month during which time Gordon started therapy. Here was the first miracle. The therapy was being done at the speech therapy center on the La Sierra campus in Riverside, and right there in Riverside resided our friend, the former mission president, Milton Neblett. He and his dear wife, Ivy, were destined to become our savior!

Since the treatment would be prolonged, Milton suggested that Gordon enroll at La Sierra College (now La Sierra University). He personally knew the dean and vouched for Gordon. He also agreed to stand as guarantor, and the dean waved the foreign student's registration fee of US $2,000! That was indeed a singular blessing! As I reflect on all that happened, I believe that God allowed Milton to live in Riverside at that time to help take care of our needs.

Milton realized that we needed transportation, and he was able to negotiate an almost new Volkswagen, UZL347, at minimal cost. This was one of the fleet of cars that the Southeastern California Conference purchased, loaned to student colporteurs during the summer, and then resold. He also knew we needed a place to live, so he bought a four-bedroom house with two full baths and a nice big kitchen, dining room, and living room in a good residential neighborhood and rented it to us and his sister, who was a graduate student of music. Then he took us to the church's Welfare Center where we outfitted our home with furniture and kitchen utensils.

Our benefactor also lent us his lawn mower and was not ruffled when we reported that someone had stolen it from the garage. He provided toy trucks for Sammy, while Ivy always invited us to lunch for Thanksgiving as well as on New Year's Day so we could see the Rose Parade on their color television. Milton and Ivy also entertained us by taking our family to Disney World in California. Our eyes opened wide as we experienced the technology

Chapter 14 Arrival in America

of the day—the animation and other activities that our minds could not grasp at the time.

Job Hunting!

We soon discovered that life in America, the earthly "promised land" where all foreigners long to inhabit, is not a bed of roses. While the opportunities exist for progress and achievement, attainment of the "American Dream" requires diligence, careful planning, hard work, and divine help. During that summer La Sierra College offered a secretarial program called "Job Readiness." On completion I was offered a job on campus, which required more skills than we learned in the short program. Also, it was a day job, and I needed to work in the evenings so I could be with the children during the day. But the course was still a blessing because it enabled me to type Gordon's thesis for his graduate degree and saved us the cost of paying professional typists whose fee was far beyond the reach of a student with a family.

Not long after, we discovered that Loma Linda University Medical Center was offering a nursing assistant training program. Even though I really did not like taking care of the sick, and I was afraid of the dead, I registered and I eventually found it to be interesting and enlightening. At the end of the program, I was employed at that institution, and I was extremely grateful to God. My first assignment was on the seventh floor, which was an orthopedic unit, and where most patients were bedridden. That meant a lot of work, but the circular formation of the rooms with the central location of the nursing station made it easy to see the patients and access their rooms. It was a delightful place to work.

It was there I met Pearl Peets from Guyana, and she gave me the orientation I needed. I noticed that the nurse in charge of the unit for the evening shift gave me the most difficult patients who needed the most care in rooms far apart from each other. More than that, she never took a report from me at the end of the shift. But God was with me. Often I would commune with Him during my dinner break. One evening she came in the nurses' lounge, and I was there on supper break, which is when I often found time to read my Bible. She was apparently shocked to see me there and made a hasty retreat. Would you believe that by the end of my first month she put in her resignation and moved to another state? It's true! "The Lord will fight for you, and you shall hold your peace" (Exod. 14:14).

Gordon continued his therapy and Esther and Sammy were usually entertained as he did his deep breathing and voice exercises. At times they even imitated his hand gestures as he repeated special passages. Here is one of them that aided both his physical and spiritual therapy.

"Often the Christian life is beset by dangers, and duty seems hard to perform. The imagination pictures impending ruin before and bondage or death behind. Yet the voice of God speaks clearly, 'Go forward!' We should obey this command though our eyes cannot penetrate the darkness, and we feel the cold waves about our feet. The obstacles that hinder our progress will never disappear before a halting, doubting spirit.... Unbelief whispers, 'Let us wait till the obstructions are removed, and we can see our way clearly;' but faith courageously urges an advance, hoping all things, believing all things" (White, *Patriarchs and Prophets*, p. 290).

Providence!

Gordon's first job on campus was in security. They nicknamed the campus police "veggie cop." He looked good in his uniform, but the income was inadequate to take care of the basic needs plus tuition. In spite of strict monetary practices, at the end of the quarter he still had a deficit. One day he received a letter reminding him that the balance was due. True, I had started to work, but I would not receive my first paycheck before the due date. If he did not pay up, he would not be allowed to take his final exams or register for the next quarter.

> *One morning in our personal devotion, we each felt impressed while on our knees to withdraw all God's tithe that we had saved and forward it that very day to the designated mission.*

Oh yes, we had some money in the bank, but it was our tithe money that we were keeping to send to Guyana at the end of the year. We didn't know what we should do. One morning in our personal devotion, we each felt impressed while on our knees to withdraw all God's tithe that we had saved and forward it that very day to the designated mission. So that day Gordon withdrew the total and mailed it immediately. When that was done, all that was left was $9.00 in our checking account. And Christmas was coming—our first in America! The children would be looking for a good Christmas dinner, a Christmas tree, and presents as they were accustomed. Our balance of $9.00 would definitely not be adequate.

On returning from work one afternoon, I found three letters in the mailbox. One was from Maisie who lived and worked in New York, another from Lyn who lived and worked in Michigan, and one from the university. Since I was sure I knew the contents of the one from the university, I left that for last. As expected, the two letters from my sisters had checks to buy something for the children. Bless you, my sisters. When I opened the one from the university my eyes opened wide! It said, "Dear Gordon: You were chosen to receive the President's award for this year to the tune of $500.00!" That was another "Praise the Lord" moment! With this grant, we were able to pay off the balance of the tuition for the quarter and a part for the next quarter. With the money from my sisters we were able to purchase a Christmas tree and some toys for both children. More than that Dr. Lyn Barker of the Kansas Avenue Church and his dear wife, whom Esther and Sammy called "Black hat teacher," invited us to have Christmas dinner with them and their three children. "What has God wrought!"

On New Year's Day Ivy invited us to watch the Rose Parade on their color TV (we had a black and white one), and then to have dinner with them. Milton and Ivy looked out for us as we struggled to plant our feet firmly on U.S. soil. He stood as guarantor for us to get credit to purchase a music console in a lovely mahogany case. That item enriched our lives in many ways. We enjoyed hours of music on Sabbath afternoons, and before bedtime the children would listen to dramatized Bible stories from the LP series called The Bible in Living Sound. Milton also surprised Gordon by presenting him with a much-needed black suit tailored by his own hands! My God, what a loving Father You are! No wonder the psalmist David burst out singing, "What shall I render to the Lord for all His benefits toward me?" (Ps. 116:12).

Chapter 15

Nursing Care Stories

Even though I preferred teaching, strangely enough I enjoyed working at the hospital. I loved meeting and talking with the patients, and I enjoyed looking for opportunities to minister to their spiritual needs. I gave the best care I could to my patients, attending to their needs—including backrubs—and offering to pray for them. I learned that prayer is a powerful tool in the hand of the Christian to minister to the sick. No one ever rejected my offer of prayer. In this way God used me to touch several lives. I am sure other nurses can share many heart-touching experiences. Here are a few of mine.

Tender Loving Care

On the orthopedic unit was a lady in her early forties who was in a whole body cast. Every day she looked out for me to visit with her and pray with her. So on my off days, I called her from my home to encourage her to put her trust in God and pray to Him. In spite of it all, she was still miserable with the cast, so eventually the doctor had it removed and she was discharged.

Then there was a young man who was the victim of a terrible accident that left him paralyzed from the waist down. As you could imagine, this was devastating for him because he had a family. At times he was very depressed. After making him comfortable for the night, I told him about God's goodness to my pastor husband with his voice problem. I told him about Timothy Greaves who also became a quadriplegic because of an accident, and how, in spite of the odds, pressed on to achieve his goal of becoming a medical doctor. Day by day I injected him with hope that often lifted his spirits. One day he happily told me that he would be able to drive a car made especially for him! I do not know what became of him because he was transferred to another unit where he could get physical therapy.

Once I was assigned to a patient who had a surgical procedure that confined her to complete bed rest. As a result when I went to attend to her, she complained of stomach discomfort due to a buildup of gas. The head nurse advised that I give her an enema, and she soon felt so relieved of her discomfort that she thanked me over and over again. One afternoon as I entered her room, I was humming the tune, "Singing I go along life's road, praising my Lord, praising my Lord, Singing I go along life's road for Jesus has lifted my load" (Eliza Hewitt, "Singing I Go," 1898).

She knew the song and joined me in singing it. As we talked she again expressed her gratitude, and when she learned that I had two small children, a son and daughter, she promised to have her daughter buy them some clothes. A day or two later she gave me a package, and when I later opened it at home, my eyes grew wide for the garments were beautiful! My marvelous God was once more telling me, "I love you, my daughter. I love you. You can trust Me." Her story had a happy ending because not long after she felt much better and was discharged.

When I discovered that I was pregnant again, I had to scale down my workload to three nights per week. So I became a "floater" and was assigned to any unit where there was a need. One night I was sent to a non-surgical unit with only one other nurse. After making rounds to make sure that all was well, I sat down, thinking that it would be a quiet night. Soon a patient's call light came on. After attending to the needs of the middle-aged woman and doing what I could to make her comfortable, I was sure she would succumb to peaceful sleep. Instead that lady virtually sat on her call button! Each time she made the same request, and each time I attended to her gently. I don't know why I didn't think of praying with her to calm her fears.

However, at the end of the shift when I was attending to her for the last time, she asked me this question, "How is it you were not annoyed with me when I called you so often?" I answered her by saying, "If you were my mother, I would want someone to take good care of her. More than that I visualized Jesus lying in the bed and thought of the care I would give to Him. What I would have done for Him I did to you." I prayed with her and never met her again. I left there hoping that my brief encounter with her would lead her to know Jesus for herself. And I remembered the words of Jesus, "Inasmuch as you have done it to one of the least of these My brethren, you did it to Me" (Matt. 25:40).

I remember the student nurse who came to work on our unit. As she moved from patient to patient, I saw her sadness, and I realized that something was weighing heavily on her mind. When she sat down to write the patient records, I seized the opportunity and began a friendly conversation with her. It is amazing that she readily unburdened her heart. She told me that she had been dating a young man for some time and he wanted to marry her. She was an Adventist Christian and he was not. She loved him but was mindful of the clear biblical warning against marriage to an unbeliever. Among other things I suggested that if she believed that God was cautioning her against marrying him, she should follow His nudging. My words had an immediate effect! Her sad countenance brightened, and a smile burst on her lips. I don't recall ever seeing her again.

Dealing With Death

Then there was an elderly male patient who raised his hand to punch me when I went to take his vital signs. I simply pulled back and reported it to the senior nurse who told me not to take it personally because he was experiencing the second stage of dying. Kubler Ross identifies those stages as follows.

- Denial—the "not me" stage. This could not be happening to me. Maybe the diagnosis is wrong.

- Anger—the "why me?" The anger is directed toward self, the world, caregivers, and God.

- Bargaining—the "I promise." If you heal me, God, I will serve You! I will do this and that.

- Depression—the "I give up" stage. The fight is over but difficult to accept, so the spirits are low.

- Acceptance—the "I accept" stage. I am resigned to my condition. I am at peace.

Do you think the apostle Paul passed through those stages while facing death at the hand of Emperor Nero? I love the words he wrote to his protégé Timothy. "I am already being poured out as a drink offering, and the time of my departure is at hand. I have fought the good fight, I have finished the race, I have kept the faith. Finally, there is laid up for me a crown of righteousness, which the Lord, the righteous Judge, will give to me on that Day, and not to me only but also to all who have loved His appearing" (2 Tim. 4:6–8). May we be ready to accept His peace which He makes available to us at all times.

One reason some people do not like to work in a hospital is that they are afraid to deal with death. Honestly speaking, I was in that group. I was so scared of dead people that I would not ride in the same elevator with that special gurney. As nurses we knew that the special gurney had a corpse on its way to the morgue. Every day I worked with the hope that I would never have to deal with one. Well, one afternoon I had to do so. He was a Hispanic male in his fifties whom we were told was in very poor health. Family members were already at his bedside when I went to take his vital signs. Not long after I left the room, the call light to his room was illuminated. He had expired! I really did not know what to do, but I gritted my teeth and decided that I had to deal with it. I was grateful when one of my colleagues came to help me and guide me through the process. She gathered up his belongings, tied his big toes together, covered his face, and called for the attendant with that special gurney.

As I took care of my other patients that day, I kept asking myself, "Why are you afraid?" The dead indeed know nothing. "The living know that they will die; but the dead know nothing" (Eccl. 9:5). Moreover, I believe in the resurrection at the second coming of Jesus when "the trumpet will sound, and the dead will be raised" (1 Cor. 15:52). Could it be that I was afraid because of the ghost stories I had heard during my childhood? Could it be that like everyone else I was just afraid of the unknown? Could it be that I still was not sure of my salvation? Whatever it is, death on the whole is a sobering moment for each one of us because in essence Jesus has come for that person.

Another difficult thing to deal with was the agony of drug withdrawal. It was terrible to hear the screams of the addict and watch his traumatic efforts to undo the restraints. Before I get self righteous, I humbly remember what Dwight Moody said when he saw the drunkard in the gutter, "There goes Moody except for the grace of God?" Then there was the man who had a terrible bout of hemoptysis. He vomited dish after dish of red blood, the result of years of cigarette smoking. As he gasped for breath, he acknowledged his error. He told of starting at an early age, ignoring the warnings of parents and friends. He wished he could live his life all over again. Then he cautioned me to never start and to warn the young of the dangers of smoking. Our gracious Father took him out of his misery soon after.

Caring for Children

Several times I was sent to the pediatric unit. It tugged at my heartstrings to see sick children with all kinds of ailments, curable and incurable. It pained me to see sick babies with encephalitis or swelling of the brain, with their heads all bandaged up. Worse of all was the twenty-five-year-old woman with the body of a six year old and severe mental retardation! She kept screaming and hitting her head against the rails of the cradle that they had padded to prevent her from hurting herself. I felt helpless. I could not touch her or talk to her or in any way ease her of her misery. On the other hand, there was a three-year-old boy with no hands—just stubs—a victim of the thalidomide drug. He stood in his cradle leaning on the rails with the sweetest smile on his face—the epitome of happiness in spite of his disabled body. No wonder I thought that Jesus spent so much time healing. His heart of love must have been pierced many times as He saw the outcome of sin.

As I looked at those sick kids, I lifted my heart and said, "Thank You, God, for giving me two healthy children." So here I want to pause in praise to God for their soundness, not only of body but of mind and of spirit. With humility, I want to salute Esther and Samuel. They were and still are simply amazing kids. They were and still are very special to me, and I love them dearly. And they loved each other growing up, and continue to do so even today. They were smart, very helpful, contented, and obedient children. They adjusted well to the move into our simple home. Since I was working the night shift, when I returned home in the morning, I needed to sleep awhile. Their instructions were to open the door to no one, and wake me if it was only quite necessary. They could look at Romper Room, a TV program similar to Sesame Street, then turn off the TV when it ended. If I was not yet awake, they could look at their books, color, or draw. And they did just as they were told! They knew that I would sleep until about noon, then get up and prepare lunch for them. Later I would read to them, and they would fall asleep in the bed together with their heads in my arms, one on each side. On Fridays they would help with house cleaning and anything else their little hands could do.

Chapter 16

Little Miracles

In Acts 12 there is an amazing story of how "an angel of the Lord" by night opened the prison doors. While I have not witnessed such a "big" miracle, I experienced many "little" ones.

God's Protection

I worked the evening shift, from 3:00 p.m. to 11:00 p.m., at the Loma Linda hospital. One night I was humming a tune while driving home when suddenly I could hardly see in front of me. I had never experienced such dense fog before, so I parked on the eaves of the road to wait it out. The man in the car behind also stopped. He told me that it was not a safe place to stay and invited me to follow him. So I did. Before I was able to reach my exit he stopped and told me that was as far as he could lead me, and after I graciously thanked him for his help, he drove on and disappeared in the foggy night. I could not understand why he left me then because we were heading in the same direction. Maybe I was driving too slowly for him.

So I continued driving slowly, wishing I had bionic eyes to pierce through the density and find my exit. Too late I realized that I had missed it! Since this was the freeway, I could not turn around. Then I remembered there was another exit with which I was not very familiar. Thank God I did not miss that one. I turned off and just followed the road. Before any anxious thought could creep into my mind, I saw young men from La Sierra

College with flashlights giving guidance to drivers. I was greatly relieved when I finally turned into our driveway. My dear husband was anxiously waiting for me. So who was the man who guided me on the highway?

On another afternoon on my way to work, I thought of using that same unfamiliar route in the daylight to better acquaint myself with it. To my surprise, I discovered that on leaving the freeway one had to make a left turn to get on the road leading to the college and to my home. But I'm sure that I did not make a left turn that foggy night! When I told Esther and Sammy the story, they instantly made up a new memory text, "The angel of the Lord by night turned Mommy's steering wheel." The miraculous experience of that foggy night has stayed with me, and it reminds me that whenever I am passing through a foggy situation in my life and am tempted to park by the side of the road, God is with me and will guide me until I reach my eternal home. And when we get there, by His grace, all the trials we experienced here on this earth will seem like nothing.

While I worked at the hospital, Gordon worked on campus in security. That required him to work the night shift, but he disliked it because he must have a good night's rest always to function adequately. So he decided to switch jobs and be the bus driver for a private church school. Then during the summer he worked as a student colporteur, something he had done before in Guyana. The training for the program was held at one of the Adventist boarding schools and families of the students were also invited. This was good since it was like a one-week vacation with all expenses paid for our family!

One morning a number of parents and children were going for a swim at the pool so they came to ask if Sammy and Esther could join them. I saw no problem since other adults would be with them, so off they went while I stayed in my room to study and pray, intending to join them later. While on my knees, I had a premonition that as soon as Sammy saw the water he would jump in and sink to the bottom, but I need not fear because someone would be there to rescue him. And believe it or not, that was exactly what happened! As soon as I reached the pool, I was told of the incident. Later on Esther told me that she too had to be rescued! She was wading and was getting deeper and deeper, but she did not understand why the water was covering her head. Slowly and imperceptibly, she was moving from the shallow end to the deep end. Miraculously, both of our beloved children were rescued that day.

> *She was wading and was getting deeper and deeper, but she did not understand why the water was covering her head. Slowly and imperceptibly, she was moving from the shallow end to the deep end.*

After his training, Gordon labored as a colporteur, working during the day and long hours into the night, but he failed to get enough sales to give him a scholarship. It was then that he decided to do the nursing program. On completion, he too was employed as a nursing assistant. He took classes in the day and worked in the evening on the 3:00 p.m. to 11:00 p.m. shift, while I changed to the "graveyard" shift as the 11:00 p.m. to 7:00 a.m. period was called. So when I was going to work, and

Chapter 16 Little Miracles

he was coming home, I would tell him "Good night!" and when I returned home from work, he would tell me, "Sleep tight!" In this way, one of us was always with the children.

God's Provision

One night while Gordon was driving home, he fell asleep at the wheel and was stopped by the police. Although he told the cops that it was because of his tiredness, he was still subjected to the heel-to-toe test to see if he was drunk. When they realized that he was telling the truth, he was given a stern warning and told not to drive when he was tired. This made us decide to move to Loma Linda. And our God had a place ready for us. Mr. Hamilton, former business manager of CUC, called "strainer" by the students, had retired, and he and his wife were living in Loma Linda. He worked at the hospital as a watchman and had a small two-bedroom property for rent. Reluctantly we left Milton Neblett's palatial house in Riverside in exchange for this small two-bedroom, one-bath house in Loma Linda. But as John Howard reminds us, "Mid pleasures and palaces though we may roam: Be it ever so humble, there is no place like home!"

One afternoon we witnessed God's provision and care for the birds. In the yard was a large walnut tree, and we saw a bird trying to get a meal from a walnut that had fallen to the ground. We doubted that the bird would be able to crack such a hard shell, but we were wrong! The tiny creature gave us a big lesson in persistence. As my mom would say, "Try, try, try again, boy [girl], you'll succeed at last!" That little bird kept rolling and pecking the walnut until it finally broke the hard shell, got its well-deserved dinner, and shared it with others. That was amazing! It reminded us of the song the children sang which said, "If God so loves the little things I know He loves me too." Jesus Himself said, "Look at the birds ... yet your heavenly Father feeds them. Are you not of more value than they?" (Matt. 6:26). So don't worry is the lesson for us humans.

However, God didn't just crack open the shell for the bird; it had to work for its food! No wonder He gave us six days to work and one day to rest. And the apostle Paul tells us that "if anyone will not work, neither shall he eat" (2 Thess. 3:10).

God's Coverage

When the sun is hot, a hat or umbrella provides covering for the head, and when the nights are cold, a blanket is needed to cover the body. When we get sick and need to be hospitalized, we also need coverage. In fact, when we call for a doctor's appointment, one of the first questions is: "What insurance do you have?" Today "Obamacare" or the "Affordable Care Act" seeks to have every citizen covered with some type of health insurance.

All was well with our family of four until one day I didn't feel well. I went to doctor after doctor. One family physician thought I was pregnant but was unsure because my menstrual cycle continued as normal from month to month. However, he told me that if at anytime I started to spot between periods I should seek immediate medical attention. One morning I awoke with pain in my upper legs. I did not feel like eating, so I went back to bed and slept for the entire morning. Even though I awoke feeling revived, Gordon thought I should still get medical attention. He told me that he had already spoken to the doctor who advised him to take me to the emergency room immediately.

But I was reluctant to go. He urged me even more when I did not eat the lunch he had provided. I just didn't feel hungry. So with our two little ones, off we went to Loma Linda Hospital. That visit was indeed providential.

An initial doctor's examination, later confirmed by a test, showed I was pregnant and the fetus was growing in the fallopian tube. If left unattended, ectopic pregnancy can cause death! This required emergency surgery. The children stood with tears in their eyes wondering what was happening to their dear mommy as they saw me wheeled away on a gurney by a male attendant. The surgery was a success, and I was back in a hospital room. Actually I was the only person in that room.

When the anesthesia started to wear off, I awoke, and feeling intense pain from the incision, I started to cry. Then I felt the presence of Jesus in the room, and He said to my heart, "Don't cry, I am here with you. Remember, the doctor told you to ask for pain medication if you needed it?" So immediately I dried my tears and called for the nurse who gave me the pain medicine that brought me much relief. As a matter of fact, God is always with us even when we don't care about Him. Remember, He told Moses to build the sanctuary in the desert so that He could "dwell among them" (Exod. 25:8). And after He commissioned the disciples, He promised, "I am with you always, even unto the end of the world" (Matt. 28:20, KJV). I like to think that even when we wander away from Him He follows in hot pursuit, hoping and waiting for us to stop, turn around, and fall right into His waiting arms of love.

Since the children were not allowed to visit me in my hospital room, I talked with them on the phone. Then when I could walk, I visited with them in the visitors' lounge. I was later told that my call was very special to Esther. She would lie on the carpet and just talk her little heart out. After about a week, I was discharged and was happy to be with my family again. That was indeed a close brush with death! Thanks to my dear husband and my heavenly Father for saving me from a possible early demise. And we did not have to pay the costs for the emergency room, surgery, and hospitalization. We were covered by Blue Cross and Blue Shield, the best health insurance coverage that the hospital provided for its employees.

And do you know that in our sin-sick world we can have the best health care insurance policy? It's available from the greatest Health Care Provider, Jesus our Savior! And it's free! We don't have to pay the penalty for our sins! Jesus paid it all with His blood! As I marvel at His gracious provision and tender care to me, these words come to mind:

Deep are the wounds transgression has made:

Red are the stains; my soul is afraid.

Oh to be covered, Jesus, with Thee,

Safe from the law that now judgeth me.

Cover with His life, whiter than snow;

Fullness of His life then shall I know;

My life of scarlet, my sin and woe;

Cover with His life, whiter than snow.

(F. E. Belden, "Cover With His Life," 1899)

Recently Betty Gordon, my prayer partner, and I were talking about the effectiveness of hymns. While some of them have theological concepts, others have heart-searching messages that reach down to the depths of the soul and drive us to make lasting decisions for Christ. One that caught my attention is:

Rock of Ages, cleft for me,

Let me hide myself in thee;

Let the water and the blood,

Chapter 16 Little Miracles

From thy wounded side which flowed,

Be of sin the double cure;

Save from wrath and make me pure.

(Augustus Toplady, "Rock of Ages, Cleft for Me," 1776)

The great thought is that the blood of Jesus not only forgives our sin and removes our guilt, but it also empowers us to overcome sin! Isn't that what we are told in 1 John 1:9? "If we confess our sins, He is faithful and just to forgive us our sins and to cleanse us from all unrighteousness." So thank You, Jesus, for both forgiving and cleansing. The pardon is complete! As Micah 7:19 says, "You will cast all our sins into the depths of the sea!" That's seven miles deep! And the change is comprehensive! Paul says, "Therefore, if anyone is in Christ, he is a new creation; old things have passed away; behold, all things have become new" (2 Cor. 5:17).

Chapter 17

Ministry in San Diego

About a year or so after that close shave, I was pregnant again. Somehow it seems that I was destined to have a third child. The miscarriage in Guyana was not the right time, and the ectopic pregnancy was evidence that that was not the right time either. And now to us, this seemed to be the wrong time. As a matter of fact, it was definitely at an "unfortunate" time. I was looking forward to the completion of both my baccalaureate and graduate degrees. We had even discussed the possibility of my studying medicine while Gordon would work. And after that we would return to Guyana to work in both pastoral and medical ministries. But somehow this child was determined not to be left out of the Martinborough tribe! So now this baby was on the way. Again, our God knew what He was doing.

"Internship" for a Senior Pastor!

When Gordon finished his first degree, he was told that the U.S. government allowed students with a J1 visa to do an internship in their area of study before returning to their home country. He wasted no time in placing his application at the Southeastern California Conference. At that very time he was told that a small church in San Diego, started by a prominent doctor, was looking for a pastor. However, there was no guarantee of employment because he would first have to be evaluated when he preached at the church. He was also told that

Chapter 17 Ministry in San Diego

others had tried, but the dear doctor was not impressed with any of them. When arrangements were made, we drove two hours in our little VW Bug to San Diego to spend the weekend at the palatial hilltop home of the prominent physician. On Sabbath morning we rode in his Lincoln Continental, and even today we still joke at how we were amazed that his garage door opened by pressing a button in his car.

The Oak Park Church had started when this physician and a few other members had a problem with the pastor of the mother church. So they withdrew and started a new church. That Sabbath spent in San Diego was the beginning of a year and half experience working with a church in the United States. And what an experience it was! The doctor later told Gordon that he was chosen because he had prepared a good sermon and under the Spirit's power had delivered it in a way that pleased the congregation. Subsequently, we were told by a friend that the physician did a background check on Gordon and she could only tell him that "he was a very hard worker."

As soon as the wife of the doctor knew of the decision and realized that we had to move to the district, she suggested that we purchase a house. Her husband would make the down payment and we would take care of the monthly mortgage. Then when we were ready to leave, they would take back the house. After an exhausting day with the realtor, we finally settled on a lovely three-bedroom house with a family room big as a ballroom and large enough to accommodate a small church. A study was next to it. It was also near a small SDA church school. We returned our home to Loma Linda, and the conference gave us the date when the truck would be available to move us to San Diego. That date happened to be before the scheduled date for the baby's arrival. My hope was that I would have the baby before leaving Loma Linda. And again God came through for us.

John's Arrival

While we waited to move, Gordon traveled to the church in San Diego, stayed over for the weekend, then returned on Sunday. It was while he was away one Friday evening that baby John was born, arriving at 12:05 Sabbath morning six years after Sammy. As I think on the birth of our three children I guess it was just coincidental that all three were born on weekends when their dad was engaged in his pastoral ministry, causing him to miss out on the excitement of the birthing process. Esther arrived at 8:30 Saturday night, and the program was Thousand Drive in Sixty Five in Guyana; Sammy, at 7:00 early Sunday morning, while his dad was doing evangelism training at Linden, Guyana; and John at 12:05 on Sabbath morning while Gordon was in San Diego. A good friend drove me to the hospital and then returned to my home to take care of Esther and Sammy who were fast asleep. Another nurse friend of mine stayed beyond her shift to see me through the delivery process. As I reflect on John's birth, it seems to me that for some reason God wanted him to be a part of our family. Could it be that he had a special plan for him in His work?

With his birth out of the way, it was easier for us to move to our new home and a new work in San Diego. Unfortunately, before we were able to move, tragedy struck the doctor's family. A fatal car accident over the mountainous highway killed his wife. The reason for such tragedies we will never know until Jesus comes. So William Cowper penned: "You fearful saints, fresh courage take; The storms you so much dread, Are big with mercy, and shall break In blessings on your head."

The house we acquired was in a predominantly white neighborhood, and we thought nothing about it. As soon as the moving van stopped at this house on the corner, the neighborhood children, curious by nature, came to look on. Their attention was directed to baby John who was only a few weeks old. As we tried settling in, we learned that one family had moved out and others planned to follow. The exodus, however, came to a screeching halt when we visited the neighbor on the left and the other across the street from us and formally introduced ourselves to them. It surely makes a difference to build bridges rather than fences.

On the other hand, the "color blind" children embraced Esther and Sammy. They played with them, taught them to skate, and taught them to swim in the family's swimming pool! Two brothers especially came to the house every day—the older built a friendship with Esther and the younger with Sammy. It seems as if the famous "I Have a Dream" speech by Dr. Martin Luther King was becoming a reality family by family. They also faced no problem at the school they attended. One afternoon we were very late in returning from Loma Linda, and the next-door neighbor took good care of Esther and Sammy. I still smile when I remember how Esther graciously refused to eat her nicely prepared liver stew that the neighbor offered them. This led her to ask us the reason. At that time vegetarianism was unpopular and was considered weird. We became good friends, and she continued to look out for Sammy and Esther.

Strangely enough, when Esther was in my womb, I once had a craving for liver. I was at the stage when my body was adjusting to the "little stranger" within, and I could not keep my food down. I bothered Gordon so much that he went and bought a half pound of the stuff. At that time we were all vegetarians, so Mom announced that she was not going to prepare it. Gordon was not willing to help either. So I prepared it myself. And I ate all of it all by myself! Not long after, the "little stranger" within sent it right back up! Maybe from then she disliked the taste. So that was the end of my cravings.

The church we were asked to pastor was a small congregation with about fifty members. So the conference assigned Gordon to work as pastor half of the time and as one of the chaplains at the Paradise Valley Hospital the other half. Just as before, Gordon and I worked as a team at the church. Every Sabbath I ministered to the children in Sabbath School, and in the worship service I gave the children's story that matched the theme of his sermon.

Evangelism at Oak Park

Since evangelism has always been a vital part of Gordon's ministry, he motivated and mobilized the church for house-to-house visitation in preparation for an evangelistic series. This unique program included a health nugget by one of the doctors and a program for the children. Well, the field was worked, the church members were assigned their different roles, and I had my creation chart ready for the children. We were as ready as we could be. But when we looked for guests on the opening night, the children came but not the parents! Gordon later discovered that the main problem was that the venue, a school building, was located in a white neighborhood. So after a week, we had to close down the campaign.

After that, the emphasis shifted to personal evangelism, and in the eighteen months we were at Oak Park, about one dozen persons were baptized. One of them later became a church elder, another became a part-time colporteur, and a third became, and still is, an effective Bible worker. One of them that

Chapter 17 Ministry in San Diego

we never forgot was a mother of four children who was on welfare. We succeeded in getting her off welfare and back to work. She found employment as a caregiver for a paralyzed Hispanic man confined to a wheelchair. And one day when she could not go, I volunteered and went to work for her so that she would not lose her job. Several years later, we were pleasantly surprised to learn of her change of status. She was married to a wealthy Caucasian who left her financially stable. Her daughter also had a stable husband.

Gradually the church grew, and so did the children and youth. The relationship between our family and the doctor's family also became stronger to the extent that at his daughter's wedding, six-year old Sammy was the Bible boy. Unfortunately, those were not the days of instant pictures so we don't have one with him all dressed up in his tuxedo looking as smart as ever!

The year and a half of "internship" was coming to an end. We would soon have to leave San Diego. But before we did Satan reminded us that he was still at work. One day as the doctor was discussing with Gordon the search for a successor, the physician asked Gordon about the experience he had working with him. In his open honesty Gordon responded that it was positive and added, "but at times I had to be cautious." That one "but" turned the tide of friendship into turmoil. The good doctor with a big bank account and a bigger ego got mad! He cut his support from the church and in a huff and puff left the small congregation to worship at another.

The devil could not have chosen a more perfect time. The church had decided to purchase a church home and the transaction was within the church's income. Now the question was "With the exit of the biggest donor, what should it do?" The president of the conference met with the members one night to find out the feasibility of the proposal. Were the members willing and able to purchase and maintain a church building without the doctor's financial input? The night of the meeting all the church members were present, and together they sealed the decision to continue with the purchase, and they received the conference's approval.

After the president left, the members stayed back to ask about the problem with the dear doctor. Remember, every story has two sides or, as some say, three sides—my side, your side, and the right side, which might be neither my side or your side. It was satisfying to note that when they heard the incident that caused the physician's tantrum, they rallied around their pastor. We later learned that the members, all African American, were amazed that a "puny black man" from a third world country could present their case so fearlessly and professionally before the white conference president. Under God the church grew, and in spite of its many challenges, it continues to the present day.

Years later when Gordon revisited the United States he attempted to reach out to the doctor, hoping to "bury the hatchet," but without success. He recently passed away. And yet on his dying bed he might have, like the thief on the cross, silently prayed, "Lord, remember me when You come into Your kingdom" (Luke 23:42).

Chapter 18

Back at Loma Linda! Providence at Work!

When our sojourn in San Diego came to an end, we returned to Loma Linda, and Gordon started working on a master's degree. Strangely enough, the director of foreign student affairs at the university did not tell us that as an experienced ordained minister with a J1 visa, Gordon could have applied for full-time work, stayed on at the church, and later have been eligible to apply for permanent residence. We were disappointed when we learned of this later on, but we came to the conclusion that if that had been God's plan for us our heavenly Father would have made it happen. After all, hadn't He worked miracles for us all along the way?

Back at Loma Linda, we found a home that was strategically located. It was not far from our workplace, the hospital; it was near the Loma Linda Elementary School for Esther and Sammy; and it was very close to a Laundromat. Gordon continued his graduate studies, and I worked at a preschool for about a year and then took a better paying job as a nursing assistant at LLUMC. I progressed with advanced training to nursing assistant levels 2 and 3. And while doing so, I took advantage of the free four credits per quarter available at either La Sierra College or Loma Linda University toward my degree in elementary education.

We Have No Money!

While we lived in that house, which is still standing today, we saw God's hand of providence at work in significant ways. One Friday afternoon before either of us received our first paycheck, we got a letter from the bank stating that there were insufficient funds in our account to make payment on one of our checks. The check had bounced! When I read it, I got mad at God! I told Him that I was done with serving Him. We were faithful in returning our tithe and in giving an offering equal to the amount of our tithe. We had labored in His work and tried to train the children to love and serve Him. I accused God of favoritism as I pointed out that others who were not serving Him were doing better than we were! I emphatically told myself that I was *not* going to prepare the Sabbath meal that Friday afternoon. And I was *not* going back to church either because He was not blessing us!

As I think about it, I was no better than the Israelites in the desert who complained about every difficulty they faced—no water and no flesh food—even though the Lord had shown His power and His protection in the crossing of the Red Sea and the destruction of the mighty Egyptians. It was always "Moses, Moses, why did you bring us here to die in the wilderness? Things were far better for us in Egypt." And here I was, mad with God over the lack of funds when the Lord had provided for us countless times before.

While I was nursing this anger inwardly, Esther and Sammy (bless their dear little hearts), were busy cleaning the house and preparing for the Sabbath. Gordon was at work, and I was engaged in no Sabbath preparation. Later that afternoon I went to take my usual evening bath, and it was then that the Lord responded with this text. He said, "Don't you know that the trial of your faith works patience? 'Let patience have its perfect work, that you may be perfect and complete, lacking nothing'" (James 1:5). Then the thought hit me, "Oh, so that's what this is! God is testing me, wanting me to be perfect!" I smile as I remember that even though I did not prepare Sabbath lunch, I did go to church the next day. And thank God, I have gone ever since that day!

As I read Scripture I realize that the psalmist Asaph had the same problem. He declared, "But as for me, my feet had almost stumbled; my steps had nearly slipped. For I was envious of the boastful, when I saw the prosperity of the wicked…. When I thought how to understand this, it was too painful for me—Until I went into the sanctuary of God; then I understood their end" (Ps. 73:2, 3, 16, 17). No wonder David urges us in Psalm 37:1–4, "Do not fret because of evildoers, nor be envious of the workers of iniquity. For they shall soon be cut down like the grass, and wither as the green herb. Trust in the Lord, and do good; dwell in the land, and feed on His faithfulness. Delight yourself also in the Lord, And He shall give you the desires of your heart." The entire psalm is worth reading.

It is also good to remember that God allows problems in our lives to correct (Ps. 119:71, 72), protect (Gen. 50:20), and to perfect (James 1:2, 3). We can sing with Andraé Crouch the hymn "Through It All" and remember God's providence even in the darkest times.

Saved From Carbon Monoxide Poisoning

Another unforgettable act of God's providence occurred one Friday night. We all went to bed early to be ready for a long trip the next day. Everyone else was sound asleep but somehow sleep eluded me. I just couldn't fall asleep! Maybe I was too tired to sleep. Amid my turning and twisting, I felt the urge to get up, and my feet led me to the kitchen and to the gas stove. And do you know what I discovered? All four knobs were turned on to full! I shudder every time I think of how God saved us all that night from sure death by carbon monoxide poisoning. That odorless gas would have killed all five of us! Were it not for the grace of God, the whole Martinborough family would have been extinct. Marco, there would not have been any Esther; no MSSNG LNKS and Sammy; no "Coming Home" CD from John; and no Happy Family Bible Seminars International for Gordon and Waveney!

> *I just couldn't fall asleep! I felt the urge to get up, and my feet led me to the kitchen and to the gas stove. All four knobs were turned on to full!*

And like David I say, "Bless the Lord, O my soul; and all that is within me, bless His holy name! Bless the Lord, O my soul, and forget not all His benefits" (Ps. 103:1, 2). Oh my God, my Father, You have been so good to me!

I want to serve You all the days of my life and be an inspiration to others. So my hymn of consecration is,

> Take my life and let it be,
>
> Consecrated, Lord, to thee;
>
> Take my moments and my days,
>
> Let them flow in ceaseless praise …
>
> Take my love; my Lord, I pour,
>
> At thy feet its treasure store.
>
> Take myself, and I will be,
>
> Ever, only, all for thee.

(Frances Ridley Havergal, "Take My Life and Let It Be," 1874)

Chapter 19

"Not Our Will, But Yours Be Done!"

Have you ever been at the crossroads? If you have, you know how challenging it is to decide which direction to choose. You look from one side to another, because each side looks like the right side. That is where we found ourselves after Gordon completed his master's degree. On one hand, we had a strong commitment to our homeland and wanted to return to serve in our country. But on the other hand, we were not yet ready to go. We wanted to stay in the United States awhile longer.

At the Crossroads!

One reason for our desire to remain was that I had not completed my degree. Since I worked while Gordon completed his degree, he wanted to work while I completed mine. A second reason we wanted to stay longer in the United States was that Guyana had become a socialist state, and the economy of the country was in shambles! Regular food items like wheat flour, split peas, and other staples were banned! Cars were sold to the privileged few. But if we stayed in the United States, our residence status had to be changed. And our friend could not come to our rescue for he was working with the federal government as a relief agent overseas. Later on he used that expertise at the world headquarters office of the Adventist Disaster and Relief Agency. So there we were standing at the crossroads.

Gordon sent out resumes, and two conferences on the East Coast showed interest. One president even called and promised to call back after meeting with his committee that very day. We waited expectantly, but no call came. Years later we learned from one of the pastors who was a member of that committee that everything was favorable until someone informed the committee of the problem that Gordon had previously with his voice. Even though this had been corrected by voice therapy, it prevented the approval.

Soon after we learned that the Southeastern California Conference was looking for an associate ministerial secretary to take care of the needs of the regional pastors, and Gordon applied. Again we were hopeful because we knew the ministerial secretary personally. He had listened to Gordon's presentations and had given positive feedback. But that did not materialize. Interestingly enough he told Gordon that he should return to his home country. We tried to get residence status on the basis of John's birth, but we were unsuccessful. My sister Maisy tried amnesty, but they took too long to respond. Then we heard of an opening at an Adventist high school and applied, but we received no answer. Gordon and I had made it a matter of prayer and fasting, but all doors seemed to close right before our faces.

The bad news that continued to come from our homeland was not only about the country but also about the church. Because of the political and economic situation, there was an exodus of talented pastors, which caused the conference to suffer from a shortage of senior pastors. And to make matters worse, one of them had suddenly died. Many were leaving, but none were returning! So after another day of prayer and fasting, the decision was made. We said, "Lord, if that is the plan You have for us, we will return home to Guyana. Not our will, but Your will be done." We decided to go and boost the work in our homeland.

After we communicated our intention to Roy, who was then the conference president, the wheels were set in motion for our return. We understood later that the Caribbean Union wanted us to go to Trinidad instead so that Gordon could be the personal ministries director of the union. We were also told that the committee viewed it with favor until someone argued that the work there needed senior workers. With that decision made, we made arrangements for the return home. As we made our travel plans, we included stops to visit my siblings in Michigan, New York, and Trinidad. Meanwhile, more attempts were made by concerned Guyanese to deter us from returning. But our decision was final. We said goodbye to the United States of America. We didn't know if we would ever return.

Gordon was assigned to Georgetown No. 1, which was the principal pastoral district of the conference, having three churches and a combined membership of 2,000, and on the first Sabbath of January 1977, we visited two of them. Carmel was a vibrant church full of young people, and our children quickly became attached to it. This church arose from an evangelistic campaign by Dr. Kembleton Wiggins, the union evangelist, and its head elder was Winston J. B. Enniss. The Central Church was the mother church. On the next Sabbath we visited the Berea Church where Ernest Burgess had served as head elder for seventeen consecutive years.

"My Heart Is Fixed!"

Now listen to this! Before leaving the United States the Lord impressed us to take out a U.S. passport for John, although he could have traveled on the passport of either of his parents. When we received the passport, we were advised by the immigration officer to register him with the U.S. embassy in Guyana as

Chapter 19 "Not Our Will, But Yours Be Done!"

soon as we arrived there. So one morning, soon after our arrival, Gordon did just that. And to our amazement, he was told that he could apply for residence status for the entire family on the basis of John's citizenship. He urged us to do so immediately, since the U.S. government would be changing that policy in another month. Once again, God was right on time! We got busy getting all the required documents and turned them in to the embassy. Then one morning at the scheduled time the whole family sat in the office of the U.S. ambassador in Guyana. First he spoke to John, then stamped the word "approved" on our papers, welcomed us as residents, and told us we were to travel to the States within a year to confirm our status. And we exclaimed, "This is the Lord's doing; it is marvelous in our eyes" (Ps. 118:23).

Remember that Guyana was in a serious downturn! The ruling government had converted it into a socialist state. Essential food items were hard to obtain. All schools had been taken over by the government. Foreign currency was controlled. Passengers traveling out of the country were searched at the airport, and any foreign currency found was confiscated. Stories of what people did and where they hid their wealth would make you blush! Electricity was in limited supply, and blackouts were prevalent. But since we were certain that it was God's will that we be in Guyana, we refused to allow these challenges to move us! We were home at God's direction. Like the psalmist we said, "My heart is fixed, O God, my heart is fixed!" (Ps. 57:7, KJV).

Part Four:

Guyana, Caribbean, and Beyond

Chapter 20

Climbing the Hill of Change

Culture Shock!

For the children, settling in this third world country was a big challenge. It was definitely a culture shock! And unfortunately as their parents we did not prepare them for it. Even we as adults who were born and reared in Guyana were not prepared for the deterioration we saw! The beautiful "garden city" of Georgetown was no longer beautiful. I was made rudely aware of the condition when one morning I took John to Bourda Market to purchase some items such as plantain, eddoes, cassava, bora (green beans), eggplant, and some luscious fruit—mangos, bananas, and pineapple. (Guyana has the sweetest pineapples you can find!)

I couldn't believe what I saw! Leaves and rotting produce laced the ground, making it slippery. The water in the trench was stagnant—a fitting breeding place for the pesky mosquitoes. This was a far cry from the verdant Bourda Market with its adjacent Bourda Green Park that we had left eight years before. The place looked bad and smelled just as bad! As we entered the market, John, in his sneakers and socks, was doing a balancing act walking on his heels, not wanting even the soles of his sneakers to be contaminated by the mess! When he could bear it no longer, the ever expressive John, who never hesitated to share his thoughts, loudly exclaimed," Mommy, you didn't tell me that Guyana was so dirty!" Unfortunately, I didn't get the point! I did not realize what the children were experiencing. Sorry, kids! We should have prepared you for changes to the country and the culture.

However, the children soon bonded with their cousins—Andre, Fern, and Faith-Ann. But for me the challenge was getting adjusted to living so close to in-laws and having none of my siblings around, whom were all in the States or England or Trinidad. Gordon was very comfortable and seemed to have completely forgotten about his wife! Several times I acted out my frustration with a tantrum here and there, but somehow it went unnoticed. And I did not know how to confront him using the "I" statements that we now teach in our ministry to families.

School for the Children

Soon it was time to register the children for school. Since there were no Adventist schools, we were directed to the primary school that had many Adventist and other Christian teachers. Then to our dismay, we were informed that Esther had to face the common entrance exam that was administered in April. And this was January! This exam was written at the end of primary school, somewhat like the FCAT done in the United States. It was designed to stream children into the various high schools. Those scoring very high points went to the best secondary schools. So Esther had four months to adjust to a new school system and prepare for this crucial exam. Basically a smart child, she attacked the school assignments with confidence, and after the exam gained a place at the once prestigious Catholic high school, St. Rose's High, where they still maintained high moral values.

For Sammy, however, the school experience was somewhat different. He was reluctant to go to school because the children taunted him, laughing at his American accent. One afternoon I kept him at home, and on the following day I visited with his teacher. Fortunately, she was a lovely, Adventist Christian lady with whom I was well acquainted. She promised to do all she could to help him adjust to the crowded open classroom school, the difference in school program, and the taunting of the children. He tried to fit in by trying to talk like his peers. Still I didn't get the point! On hindsight, in addition to encouraging him, I should have challenged him to be unafraid to be himself.

In spite of it all, Samuel settled down and did very well in school. More than that, at church he taught the primary Sabbath School class and was active in Pathfinders. It was there at Carmel that he showed leadership qualities. He was a member of a junior male quartet, and although he was not the oldest, I was told that he often called them to prayer especially when they had to sing. This was made evident at one of the national music competitions. Their quartet was the last to be called to render their selection.

Since it was their first appearance before a community audience, I felt a slight flutter at the pit of my stomach. If they were anxious, they did not show it because they sang with God-given confidence. This was the result of practice and prayer. The song they sang was a favorite of mine. We all listened and waited for them to get to the last line. And when young Enniss with his deep bass voice came in at the right time and hit the right note, the hall erupted in cheers. They won outright! With their faces aglow, they found a quiet spot to give praise to the "Source" of their success.

Esther also led out in various activities, and since she played the piano, she was eventually appointed to be the leader of the church choir, which consisted of both youth and adults. She too exhibited leadership skills at an early age.

Chapter 20 Climbing the Hill of Change

Could you imagine a teenager openly challenging the views of the music director of the Caribbean Union? Well, isn't her name Esther? She was so named because she was born at the height of the "Thousand Drive in Sixty Five" initiative. As we thought of a name and remembered the incidents of her birth, Mordecai's famous question to his cousin Hadassah came to mind, "Who knows whether you have come to the kingdom for such a time as this?" (Esther 4:14). And so we named her Esther. She blessed all with her music, and her efforts paid off when, with a team of other young people, she planned and executed a concert that filled the 300-seat YWCA auditorium to overflowing. It was there that John made his public debut and brought down the house with his song "Joy in the Morning!" Tough as it was, Guyana was a blessing to both Esther and Sammy. It set the stage for an excellent work ethic that propelled them into their future. We praise God for being with us in those difficult times.

Four-year-old John was home schooled. When he was not trying to sound out his letters to read phonetically, he would sing his soul out on the veranda. That prompted our neighbor to call him Johnny Mathis. Just like his siblings, Johnny started school at age seven and was accepted at St. Margaret's, one of the highly appraised primary schools in the city. The principal was reluctant to put him in the grade with those of his own age, and started him at the first grade. However, at the end of the first quarter, he was promoted to second grade, and at the end of the school year, he was successful and moved up to the third grade. When he took the common entrance exam a year early, he qualified to attend Queen's College. However, we chose St. Rose's High School, which still maintained the moral values that attracted us to it in the first place. This was the alma mater of both Esther and Sammy.

Chapter 21

Shepherdess in Georgetown 1 District

The Shepherdess

Since Gordon was a shepherd of the flock in the city, I was a shepherdess. In fact, as I look back over the years, regardless of my familial or professional roles, I have always been a partner with my husband in ministry. When we served in Georgetown, I was able to make significant contributions. At that time I was a stay-at-home mom with John and available to help Sammy or Esther whenever they needed help with school assignments. In addition, I was actively ministering in the three churches of our pastoral district—Central, Berea, and Carmel.

I served as Sabbath School superintendent at Carmel and challenged members to early Sabbath School attendance by starting promptly on time. Persons on the program who came late did not participate because, as the saying goes, "Time and tide wait on no man." And that strategy worked. Little by little Sabbath School filled up as members came early. (Today we need strategies to encourage attendance at Sabbath School.)

Then I was asked to sponsor the Missionary Volunteer Society, now YAM, to work with the young people of all three churches. With a team of young people, we planned programs and activities for all-round development. One Sabbath afternoon every month, the youth from the three churches met in one of the churches for a joint MV program. For the preliminaries we promoted memorization of scripture texts from the Morning Watch calendar, engagement in missionary work, and programs for higher education. The quote "Higher than the highest human thought can reach is God's ideal for His children" was the motivating factor (White, *Education*, p. 18). The main part of the program was a series of skits based on some of the reformers who I had researched and prepared skits for.

Drama of the Reformers

The first character we dramatized was John Wycliffe who is called the Morning Star of the Reformation. He fearlessly preached against the mendicant friars and the money-loving monks. Wycliffe challenged papal authority and upheld the supremacy of Scripture. When he got sick and they thought he was going to die, the priests visited him and urged him to recant. The drama in the MV presentation was very effective as the costumed youth who played the role of Wycliffe rose from his bed (a hospital cot) and pointing to the prelates said, "I will not die, but live; and again declare the evil deeds of the friars." He lived, and along with his associates translated the Bible from Latin into English, producing the first English Bible called the Wycliffe Bible. Since then many have followed in his steps so that we now have the Bible in a variety of translations.

We also dramatized the martyrs Huss and Jerome. John Huss of Bohemia became a disciple of Wycliffe and opposed the sale of indulgences for the remission of punishment for sin. He was arrested and imprisoned, and when he failed to recant, he was burned at the stake! As the flames curled around and engulfed him, he sang to the glory of God! At first Jerome recanted under pressure and fear of the furnace, but later, realizing how he had dishonored his Lord, he bravely requested that his hands be burned first for cowardly signing the papers of renunciation. As we envisioned these scenes, we all wondered if we could sing under pain of death. I believe that God was with these martyrs somehow numbing their pain and that He will do the same for anyone who has the faith and courage to stand up for Him.

Another inspiration was Martin Luther, the German reformer who defied the might of Rome and nailed his ninety-five theses to the chapel door at Wittenberg. He felt urged to do so as Tetzel sold indulgences. The saying was, "As soon as the coin in the coffer rings, the soul from purgatory springs." As he stood before the Diet of Worms in defense of his faith, he was questioned, "I ask you, Martin—answer candidly and without horns—do you or do you not repudiate your books and the errors they contain?"

To this Luther replied, "Since then Your Majesty and your lordships desire a simple reply, I will answer without horns and without teeth. Unless I am convinced by Scripture and plain reason—I do not accept the authority of popes and councils, for they have contradicted each other—my conscience is captive to the Word of God. I cannot and will not recant anything, for to go against conscience is neither right nor safe. God help me. Here I stand, I cannot do otherwise."

The last reformer that we dramatized was the young Scottish reformer, John Knox. It was he who earnestly prayed, "Give me Scotland, or I die!" He was instrumental in replacing Catholicism with Protestantism in Scotland. Those were men of courage, fearless like Paul and Silas singing in prison with their feet in those uncomfortable stocks and their backs lacerated from the floggings received from the Roman whip. They were calm and unafraid like Peter sleeping in prison, chained to his guards, knowing that the next day he would be facing the execution block. Today we too need to know what we believe, in whom we believe, and stand up for what we believe. Either we stand up for something, or we will fall for anything!

On the final Sabbath afternoon of our MV meetings, as we assembled at the Central Church, the Spirit of the Lord was surely in that place! At the close I felt inspired to challenge the youth to stand with me and declare their desire to do and dare for God. Even today in my mind's eye I can still see Central Church packed to capacity. As I write I am still thrilled at the thought of both young and old standing spontaneously in response to the call as we sang the hymn, "Faith of our Fathers." It was an electrifying moment!

> Faith of our fathers! living still,
>
> In spite of dungeon, fire, and sword;
>
> Oh, how our hearts beat high with joy
>
> Whene'er we hear that glorious word!
>
> Faith of our fathers, holy faith!
>
> We will be true to thee till death!
>
> (Frederick W. Faber, 1849)

Imagine the impact as we sang the chorus again and again—an idea I got from the saintly Pastor Ivan Berkell when he was my pastor. Gordon later told me that if I had made an altar call for baptism, I would have had a tremendous response.

A Spectrum of Activities

The last drama we presented was "Are you a Jeannie?" The intent of this production was to alert our young people of their need to know what they believed and be able to defend their faith before a judge by showing from Scripture the reason for their beliefs. It was also to help them realize that regardless of their judicious defense they could be imprisoned, but they would not be left alone because they were under the watch care of their unseen angels. And beyond that, when Christ comes again, prison doors would be opened at the sound of the trumpet and Jesus would take them to His heavenly home. Only eternity will reveal the impact of these programs on the hearts of those young people.

Social activity for the youth took various forms. There were indoor and outdoor games as well as movie nights. Before returning to Guyana we had bought a movie projector, and so we were able to look at a variety of movies. At the end of the year we planned a year-end couples' banquet with the theme "Under the Ocean." With the guidance of the young ministerial intern, Winston Albert, the young people used their imagination in decorating the lower flat of Carmel Church.

One Mothers' Day the youth were encouraged to have a "shut-in visitation day" instead of the regular MV meeting. They were asked to visit and bring cheer to the elderly at their homes or wherever they were and minister to them. I doubt they were enthused with the idea, but nevertheless they followed through with it. At the end they returned rejoicing and willing to testify of the blessing they received.

It was really a delight to minister to the children during the worship service where young and old alike waited for the children's story. Today it is sometimes called children's chapel. But I did not tell just any story. Instead, I would get the sermon topic from my husband and use a story that matched the theme of the sermon. The folk at Central Church simply loved it. And I loved the challenge of not only finding the story, but also presenting it in an interesting way. I also enjoyed working as the head usher in major evangelistic programs.

After a large evangelistic program, the newly baptized members were still worshiping under the tent. One Sabbath morning when it

Chapter 21 Shepherdess in Georgetown 1 District

was the time for the Sabbath School lesson, it was discovered, much to the dismay of all, that no one was assigned, and none of the young pastors was willing to do it at a moment's notice. So guess what? Gordon asked me to fill the gap. And the Spirit of the Lord was with me! He guided me through the lesson step by step. He even reminded me of one of my own experiences at the appropriate time to illustrate an important point—the role of the law and grace.

> *I did a rolling stop at the stop sign after a quick glance showed that the road was clear of any oncoming traffic. As I rounded the corner there was a policewoman waiting for lawbreakers like myself!*

I told of how I was driving home from the market one day and how I did a rolling stop at the stop sign after a quick glance showed that the road was clear of any oncoming traffic. As I rounded the corner there was a policewoman waiting for lawbreakers like myself! My heart sank when I saw her. She stopped me and proceeded to look into the car. Before she could open her mouth to speak, I said, "I am at your mercy!"

She looked at me and sternly asked, "What did you say?" I repeated my plea for mercy. After looking around in the car and seeing my purchases, she let me go. And oh how grateful I was! That was grace! I did not deserve her letting me off without writing me a ticket.

"So tell me," I continued, "did the grace I received that day do away with the law? Did it give me permission to ignore the stop signs and break the law again and again because of the grace I received? Of course not! You would agree that the proper response of grace is repentance, gratitude, and a turning away from the wrong. So when we are saved by the grace of God, we do not reject the law of God as some folk say. Come to think about it, if there is no law, there is no need for grace! The apostle Paul makes it clear when he asks, 'What shall we say then? Shall we continue in sin that grace may abound? Certainly not!' (Rom. 6:1, 2). So the Ten Commandments, including the Sabbath, is still binding on every human being today." And everyone said, "Amen!"

As I review the past, I pause to praise God for the varied gifts He gave me and the ability to use them to His glory. As a result I have come to agree with the statement that our "God is not looking for your ability, but your availability."

Chapter 22

Back to the Workplace

St. Pius Government School

It was Solomon, the wisest man, who said, "There is a season, a time for every purpose under heaven" (Eccl. 3:1). For me the time to be at home was over, and it was time to go back to work. John was now in school, so I went searching for a job. I was interviewed for high school employment, and while waiting for a response one of my church sisters told me of an immediate opening at St. Pius Primary, which was formerly a Catholic school. The principal was delighted at my experience and hired me on the spot. I started the next week.

Early Monday morning I made my way to the school and was assigned to the third grade, known as standard one in Guyana. The children were a reflection of the neighborhood from which they came. Their ability to learn was hindered by their inability to listen and obey. I discovered this on my very first day. At about 10:00 a.m., after doing reading and math, we had recess. All was well until I tried to get them back into class. Those children refused to listen and just went on playing. And when I finally got them back in the schoolroom, there was bedlam! They just would not settle down. Since the school had open classrooms, I had to maintain order so as not to disturb the other classes. As I looked around, I saw the teacher of the nearby class with a switch. I borrowed it from her and hit the desk once or twice with it. And silence reigned!

Good! I thought. Then I took advantage of the situation and had them stand at attention

Chapter 22 Back to the Workplace

without movement for a minute or two. There they were with their hands at their sides daring not even to blink! I had to show them once and for all who was in charge. And they got the message. They finally settled down and we were able to resume the next lesson after I gave them a pep talk on behavior that is conducive to learning. After that I had no more problems. And I did so without actually using the switch on any of them. I had pledged that I would not use corporal punishment on any child. Why? I had three children of my own. More than that, I loved those twenty-five kids and wanted to make a difference in their lives.

> *As I looked around, I saw the teacher of the nearby class with a switch. I borrowed it from her and hit the desk once or twice with it. And silence reigned!*

As time went on I would tell them Bible and other character-building stories. I often told them that they were human beings with brains to be used and not donkeys to be driven with a whip. I was delighted at their improvement and their attention to the class assignments. I felt rewarded when at the end of the school year we were able to promote most of them. One day the teacher whose chair was back to back with mine, said, "Miss, I have to admit that you really worked with these children." Often in my reflective moments I think about them and wonder what became of them. Only eternity will reveal the outcome of my efforts with those kids. What a thrill it would be to see some of them in the kingdom!

I looked forward to staying at St. Pius for a long time, especially when in my second year a pupil teacher was assigned to me. This brilliant young man, Andre Clark, lived in the neighborhood and was successful at the Senior Cambridge examination. Even though I had not met him before, he was a member of one of the churches in our pastoral district. He and Janice, who later became his wife, became my very good friends, and that friendship continues to this day.

This partnership continued through the first quarter of the new school year. We now had a new group of third graders. These were bright-eyed and eager to learn, and I looked forward to teaching them that year. However, God had other plans for me. Toward the end of the quarter I was invited to be chaplain of the sixty-bed Davis Memorial Hospital. Although this was something new and different, it afforded me the opportunity to continue my service record with an Adventist organization. So I had to say goodbye to St. Pius.

From Educator to Hospital Chaplain

I knew about working in the classroom and I loved teaching, but I knew nothing about hospital chaplaincy. True, I had developed a liking for hospitals from working at LLUMC. But this was different! However, when we realize our need and ask God for help, He gives wisdom and guidance and rewards our efforts. He directed and helped me to serve successfully. My responsibility was not only to minister to the patients but also to the staff of the institution. One of the vehicles for giving spiritual help to the workers was the daily morning worship services.

We did a series on the stories behind the psalms of David. We also adopted the Prayer at Noon activity, which was promoted by the Guyana Conference. Here we prayed for the doctors, as well as for increase in patient count, which at times would reach as low as seven. Gordon, now president of the conference, presented a week of spiritual emphasis. The interesting topics like "Room 9: Isolation" and others caused the worship room to be filled to overflowing. We closed that week with a Friday night communion service. We also celebrated special Sabbaths at the hospital site. As usual, the day's program had Sabbath School and a worship service in the morning, and this was followed by lunch for everyone. In the afternoon we distributed health magazines in the surrounding community and had skits or frank discussions on relationships at all levels—administrator, doctor, nurse, and patients.

The mission story for Sabbath School took the form of a skit that showed how the hospital came to be named "Davis Memorial." The story dated back to 1910 when Pastor O. E. Davis, superintendent of the then British Guiana Mission, pioneered the work among the Amerindians living in the interior of the country. After months of hazardous travel, he finally reached Mt. Roraima. As the story goes, he met the village chief who related a dream in which he was told to change his lifestyle by temperate living, keeping the Sabbath, and using only clean foods. As a result of the efforts of this Adventist pioneer, the chief and others were converted. Unfortunately, Elder Davis, weakened by the trip, succumbed to malaria and was buried there. The Arecuna and Akawaio tribes among whom he worked have been called the "Davis Indians," and the work continues to grow among these tribes to this day. The hospital was named in honor of this pioneer.

I believe that one of the many gifts that God has given me is the ability to adjust to new situations, to take up a challenge, learn to like it, and move it forward. And that is what happened at Davis. Have you ever heard that if God brought you to it He will carry you through it? I had not been a chaplain before, but He guided me in that responsibility. I listened to the hurts and dealt with wrongs of the workers. I prepared a monthly bulletin board with a theme, thought-provoking quotations, birthday acknowledgments, and interesting articles. At Christmas time we had a party and gift exchange among workers.

The matron and I developed a nursing assistant curriculum for training interested young people to do simple duties around the hospital. From this humble beginning, one student went on to pursue a degree in medicine, another completed a degree in nursing, and others pursued other health-related programs. One was later appointed conference health director, and another went to CUC to pursue a course in business administration and later became the treasurer of that institution.

This story might not be considered significant in these days, but it was when it happened in those days. Our doctor was told of a woman who had suffered from a problem for years, and no physician was able to help her. She came to DMH, and after listening to her symptoms, our physician decided to do exploratory surgery. To his amazement he discovered the bones of a decomposed fetus from an earlier miscarriage! He reconstructed the bones and showed them to me. The lady's problem was solved, and she was extremely grateful.

Service to Patients

My daily routine involved visiting patients; listening to their expressed needs, cares and concerns; and praying with them. It also included observing those who showed an interest in spiritual things, visiting them after they

Chapter 22   Back to the Workplace

were discharged, and conducting Bible studies in their homes. On one of my rounds I met a lady who was a Jehovah's Witness. She told me that she had joined that faith because she believed that God sent one of their members in answer to her prayer at the time when she asked Him to send someone to visit her that day. This confirmed, to me, the blessing of visiting people in their homes.

On my rounds I met gold miners who suffered with cramps as a result of deep river diving. I also met a demon possessed young woman who tossed the Bible someone placed on her chest. Some staff members called me to pray for her. I took one look at this woman and decided that I was not ready to deal with that case. I was too drained from listening and trying to understand the problems of other patients. I was relieved when her mother realized the nature of her daughter's problem and asked for her release. We do not know what became of her.

I will always remember Mr. X, the patient who was the owner of a music band. After being healed of leprosy, he had formed a famous music band that played for various functions. His wife and daughter were Adventists, but he was not. At his request I studied with him in his room every day at 10:00 a.m. and tried to answer his many questions. Many times I saw the Holy Spirit bring conviction to his heart. Many times I prayed that he would allow the Healer of all diseases to cure him of spiritual leprosy. Many times he spoke of his convictions, but he could not bring himself to make that decision. He confided that his main concerns were for his band members. After he left the hospital, I visited him at his home. His dear wife and daughter were hopeful.

One Monday morning when I arrived at work, I saw a covered corpse just outside my office door. That was where the deceased were placed as the bodies awaited pick up by the funeral home. It was Mr. X! I was told that he had been out with his band, felt ill, and was rushed to the hospital where he died soon after. My heart sank! His grieving daughter asked if I was there to hear his last words. But unfortunately, since it was during the weekend, I had not been present. I hope that he gave his life to his Savior before he passed away.

Then there was Aunt J who was in and out of hospital. She was a devout Catholic and highly recognized in her church and society. When we met she told me that the chaplain before me had worked with her. After additional Bible study and prayer, she finally requested baptism. I arranged a special service for her, and when she came out of the pool she shouted, "I am healed! I am healed!" This caused me to wonder about her true motive for baptism. Was she using it to gain God's favor to perform a miracle for her healing? Strangely enough, her final rites were administered by her former church.

In one of the reserved hospital rooms was a burly and somewhat wealthy gold miner who, after I visited and prayed with him, requested Bible studies at his home. It was there I met his lovely wife and three children aged thirteen, ten, and eight. She was a former Adventist who had slipped away because of her marriage. At the end of several weeks of study, they all decided to give their lives to Jesus and to demonstrate it by baptism. As usual I made the necessary arrangements with the pastor of a church that was very near to their home. On the scheduled Sabbath, the wife and the two teens were baptized. But where was the husband? He was at home suffering from a bout of anxiety that manifested itself in frequent trips to the bathroom!

The strange thing was, as he stated afterward, that he could hear the church service, including the sermon, from his window. Our gracious God used the wind to carry the message right where he was! He was then further convinced, and the next Sabbath he followed Jesus in baptism. I continued to visit the family to strengthen and encourage them in the faith. He even started a steel orchestra with the young people of his church. I lost contact with them after they moved away to a district in the county of Essequibo far from the city where I lived. I hope to meet them in God's kingdom.

There was an Adventist lady whom we were certain was nearing death. When I visited her she was unconscious and her family was at her bedside. Before I left for home that afternoon, I stopped by to encourage and pray with the family. They requested that we sing,

> The great Physician now is near,
>
> The sympathizing Jesus;
>
> He speaks the drooping heart to cheer,
>
> Oh! hear the voice of Jesus.
>
>
> Sweetest note in seraph song,
>
> Sweetest name on mortal tongue,
>
> Sweetest carol ever sung,
>
> Jesus, blessed Jesus!
>
> (William Hunter, "The Great Physician," 1859)

When I arrived the next morning, I did not see the bed with the covered corpse at my door, so I hurried to her room. The dear sister was sitting in bed having breakfast! They later told me she had been in a diabetic coma and the treatment she received along with the prayers offered on her behalf had been very effective. Thank God, she left the hospital a few days after. The Bible says, "Is any among you sick? Let him call for the elders of the church, and let them pray for him ... And the prayer of faith will save the sick, and the Lord will raise him up" (James 5:14, 15).

I cannot resist telling the story of the twelve-year-old boy who was rushed to the hospital about 6:00 p.m. with a knife in his chest. Everyone sprang into action! Fortunately, the knife, even though very close to his heart, did not puncture it. Surgery was performed to remove the foreign object, and day after day he was the subject of our intense prayer as he slipped in and out of consciousness. Our gracious God heard our prayers, and the Great Physician was by his bedside. Day by day as he improved he would greet us with a big smile. After several weeks he was discharged. He had become the prized patient of the doctor and the joy of all who helped in his miraculous recovery. To God be the glory!

Chapter 23

Multiplied Miracles in Guyana Conference

At the conference session of 1980 Gordon was elected president of the Guyana Conference, and shortly after, Roy his predecessor and his family left for Andrews University. In the country things went from bad to worse, and regular barrels of commodities entering the country duty-free from relatives in the United States became a lifeline for some people. And we joined the list of recipients! Every now and then, sometimes at just the right time, a barrel of food supplies would arrive from one of my sisters in the United States. And when we made our annual trips to the States, we benefitted from their generosity. In New York Maisie supplied the necessary U.S. currency to help us purchase much-needed items for the children. Even Mom, who had become a U.S. resident, gave us what she could from her limited social security income. Thank you, my dear sisters, for your acts of love. And once again we praise You, O Lord, for Your lovingkindness to us, Your children.

Whenever we returned home, we had to face the customs' officials who diligently searched the luggage of nationals leaving and returning to Guyana. New clothing or electronic items were heavily taxed. So before leaving the United States we made sure we opened and discarded each price tag and every wrapping of the new clothes and shoes that we were able to purchase for our three children, and made them look like they were used. As the saying goes, "The stricter the government the wiser the population." A few times we even dared to take in electronic devices and somehow we were always able to pass without having to pay exorbitant duty on those items. Our God protected us.

Prayer Action Objectives

While I was busy at DMH, Gordon was grappling with his herculean task as conference president. He had limited resources but was blessed with a cadre of young energetic workers, recent graduates of Caribbean Union College and Andrews University. Like Nehemiah of old he began with prayer. Under divine inspiration and with a team of administrators and departmental directors, a strategic plan was developed and shared with the membership of the conference at the various district conventions. At the top of the list was the daily Prayer at Noon program.

Each month focused on a different challenge that the Guyana Conference was facing, and this was called a Prayer Action Objective. All around the country members stopped at noon each day to pray for the assigned objective. This was also observed by the workers at the conference office, as well as by employees at Davis Memorial Hospital. The popular saying is true, "Many things are wrought by prayer than the world dreams of." Our prayer-hearing God heard and answered the prayers of the saints. He says in Psalm 50:15 "Call upon Me in the day of trouble; I will deliver you, and you shall glorify Me." We look back with nostalgia and praise God for the multiplied miracles He performed.

One of these objectives was GAME. Once a year we had to travel to the States to satisfy the requirement for U.S. residence status, and Gordon used the opportunity to meet with Adventist Guyanese living in New York and California to solicit their financial support for the conference. Our first stop was New York. They were very interested to hear of the state of the country and the work of the conference. It was at one of these meetings that the idea was born to form the Guyana-American Missionary Endeavor (GAME), and Winston J. B. Enniss, the former head elder of Carmel, was the first president. This fundraising initiative exists to this day and has blossomed into weekend or one-day conventions in a variety of locations around North America. Another miracle was the setting up of a U.S. account at the head office of the Inter-American Division (IAD) in Miami. This was suggested by Maxwell Blakeney, the then administrator of DMH, and the division agreed to the proposal. This meant that members and friends in the United States could send their financial support for the conference to the IAD, and these funds could be used in the United States to make needed purchases for the conference. This was extremely useful at that time because of the strict foreign exchange restrictions that had been imposed by the Guyana government. That account exists up to this day.

The ownership of a printing press was another miracle. Since we could not get foreign exchange from the government to purchase books and Sabbath School quarterly study guides, which were printed abroad, there arose the need for a conference-owned printing press. We learned that God likes us to ask Him for big things. As someone said, "Attempt great things for God and expect great things from God." And we also discovered that God puts persons in our paths to get these things accomplished! My brother Aubrey was a catalyst that God used. He introduced us to a friend Carl Hinds, who directed us to the publishing director of the General Conference, who guided us and aided us with the process and the purchase. And with U.S. donations and duty-free provisions of

Chapter 23 Multiplied Miracles in Guyana Conference

the Guyana government, the dream became a reality! The prime minister was present at the dedication of the facility, and the printing needs of the conference were supplied. Although it no longer fills a vital role, it still operates today.

A fourth miracle was the purchase of motor vehicles. The economic decline took its toll on the transportation system of the country and mobility was challenging. This added to the stresses of district pastors who could not afford to own their own cars. While the government did not release foreign exchange to do such purchases, it granted duty-free concession to any vehicle that we could bring in. So as U.S. funds became available, the conference purchased cars for pastors. Those who benefitted from this blessing made monthly payments with local currency. Using this procedure, and with the aid of Dr. Samuel DeShay, we were able to purchase and outfit a mobile health unit that was used by both the conference and the hospital. As chaplain I was able to use it several Sabbaths to take nurses to different areas of the country to hold worship services, conduct health screenings, and present health lectures.

East Indian Evangelism

One of our Prayer Action Objectives was East Indian evangelism. Of the six races of Guyana, Blacks and East Indians were the two largest segments. The Indian population was made up of Muslims and Hindus, and there were very few Indian Adventists. So the conference identified a few competent Indian lay preachers and invited them to become paid lay evangelists to conduct evangelistic campaigns in the heavily-populated East Indian areas and nurture the new congregations. At the hospital Dr. Ranju Prakasam, an Indian national, joined our staff, and the conference enlisted her in its special outreach.

Just about that time Pastor Justin Singh from India joined the staff of the Caribbean Union, which is headquartered on the nearby island of Trinidad. So he was invited to conduct a couple of campaigns in the Indian strongholds of Guyana. He and his wife arrived wearing their national Indian costumes, and they brought with them Indian musical instruments that were played to accompany the Bhagans which they sang. It was a new experience for evangelism in Guyana! As a result of his campaign held at La Bonne Intention (LBI), God blessed with the baptism of forty-six Indian converts, and with the aid of donations, a church building was erected. Thank God that church still exists today, and a large new elegant edifice is now under construction. In his campaign at Belvedere, Corentyne, fifty-two souls were baptized and a new church established.

I liked the idea of a joint ministerial retreat at the Goshen youth camp. The pastoral families of neighboring Surinam were invited to join with our pastors and our new Indian lay evangelists along with their families. I had the responsibility for the shepherdess sessions for the pastors' wives. There was time for recreation and relaxation, and there was time for prayer and spiritual renewal. At the vesper's service on Sabbath afternoon, Philip Joseph, a promising young East Indian lay evangelist, gave the message. We were all impressed with his presentation, and I was pleasantly surprised to hear Esther, a junior in high school, sing a solo for the first time. The song he had requested of her was "The Lighthouse," which had been made popular on the album of the famous Del Delker. I questioned whether there was something developing with those two young people as I saw them often in each other's company. Sadly, tragedy struck soon after.

It was a Sunday night, and we were already in bed when the phone rang. The sad voice on the other end said, "Elder, there's bad news! There was a fatal accident with the jeep, and Phillip was its victim!" Gordon hurriedly dressed and drove the fifteen miles to the crash site on the East Coast Demerara and picked up the lifeless body of this dear young man. The driver and some others were injured and all went to DMH. The life of this young worker who was scheduled to attend CUC later that year had been extinguished. That tragedy brought great sadness to our hearts and raised the age-old question "Why?" A friend of the deceased was so perturbed that he said, "Pastor, we must have faith. Let us go to the morgue and earnestly pray, asking God to raise him as He did Lazarus of old!"

Several months after the burial, we heard the good news that Phillip's mother, who had been diametrically opposed to her son's call to ministry of the church that she claimed had "killed her son," eventually gave her life to Jesus and was baptized. She died a faithful member. Can you imagine the meeting and the greeting in the new earth between mother and son? My God, You are a good God!

East Indian evangelism was only a part of the evangelism drive of the conference. All over the country willing lay preachers were trained, motivated, and supplied with their books of "New Life" sermons free of charge. Under the power of the Holy Spirit, and with the support of their pastors, they saw hundreds of souls baptized each year. Guyana became the leading conference for lay evangelism in the Caribbean Union!

Yes, those were difficult days politically, economically, and socially, but they were exciting days for the onward march of the church. Clergy and laity prayed together and worked together, reaching and surpassing evangelistic targets and Ingathering goals. As in the days of Nehemiah, "everyone had a mind to work," and under God the work in Guyana prospered. It was simply a thrill to listen to annual reports of the pastors. And at the midyear and year end meetings of the Caribbean Union in Trinidad, the report from the Guyana Conference was always the highlight. Everyone wanted to hear of the goodness of the Lord in the difficult land of Guyana.

"Here Am I, Send Me!"

As we reminisce we can only exclaim, "What has God wrought!" And to think of it, Gordon was not interested in being president! On one hand as a senior pastor he knew he could make a difference, but on the other hand he felt that he was inadequate for the task of serving as president. He was then serving as personal ministries director of the Caribbean Union, and the union's lay preachers were on the march! He enjoyed lay evangelism training, but he did not think he was equipped for or would enjoy administration. So like Jonah, he tried to run away! But the hand of God was upon him! While he did not end up in the belly of a fish, he did end up on the bed of a hospital. And here's the story. A few months after his election to the presidency of the Guyana Conference, we traveled to the 1980 session of the General Conference of the world church, which was held in Texas. All presidents were official delegates. This was the first GC session that we ever attended, and we were amazed at all that transpires at such a convocation. As we wandered around visiting the various booths, we signed up for free health checks, including blood tests. When we got the result, it showed that Gordon's hemoglobin (HB) was extremely low, with a reading of 7! They advised him to see his doctor as soon as possible. But we were not returning home immediately after. We had arranged to ride a bus with church members going to Washington, D.C. where some of our family members lived. We drove all night and in the mid afternoon arrived at Washington Adventist Hospital where both Aubrey and Joyce worked.

We must have looked like vagrants because while we waited in the lobby we both fell asleep until we were rudely awakened by security who wanted to know what we were doing there. On learning who we were, they were ready to accommodate us, and soon Aubrey and Joyce appeared to take us to their home. All went well until the night of Ray's recital at his school. While there Gordon complained of feeling ill and soon fainted. When I told Aubrey about the low blood count, he took him to the hospital, stayed by to get the blood work done, and reported the results to the doctor. Gordon was admitted, and the next day he received one to two pints of blood.

While awaiting the diagnosis, Gordon bargained with the Lord! If this was something serious, he would decline the appointment to the presidency! So when the diagnosis was completed, and it was clear that this was not a life-threatening condition, he knew beyond all doubt that God had refused to release him. Like Moses of old, his excuses had been silenced! So like Isaiah he finally submitted and declared, "Here am I Lord, send me." And believe it or not, as soon as that submission was made, peace filled his soul and plans flooded his mind! During that recuperation period in the hospital, he started to frame vital strategies for the conference. It was while there that Aubrey introduced him to Carl Hinds, and from the hospital he went straight to the office of the General Conference publishing director to start laying plans to acquire a printing press for the conference! So we can truly say, "This is the Lord's doing, and it is marvelous in our eyes!" To God be the glory!

Chapter 24

More Drama in Guyana

At the Crossroads Again!

Gordon served for two three-year terms as conference president, 1980 to 1986. But the second term almost did not happen! In 1982 the Caribbean Union session convened. The Caribbean Union extends from the British and U.S. Virgins in the north to Trinidad and Tobago in the south. As we arrived for the session in Trinidad, the rumor was that several of the young pastors wanted Gordon to be the new union president. What was being done in Guyana had caught the attention of many who saw him as the most likely candidate. The Guyanese pastor who was my informant told me, "Sister Martinborough, the buzz is pastor for the presidency. It is serious, and I am afraid."

And indeed Gordon was nominated. However, besides his love for Guyana, he believed that he did not have the experience for leadership of the union since he had not yet completed a term as a conference president. So when his name came up for review, he asked the presiding chairperson to withdraw his name from the list. The members of that nominating committee were stunned, because they knew—though he did not—that the presidency was within his grasp. On one hand pastors and workers from the other territories who greatly desired his leadership loudly voiced their dissent and asked the question "Why?" But the Guyana delegation was greatly relieved. One expressed it in typical Guyanese lingo, "If Pastor Martinborough was elected and had to

Chapter 24 More Drama in Guyana

leave the Guyana Conference, I would a buss cry!" meaning "I would burst into tears and cry out!"

Many times in our reflective moments together we have both wondered if it was an error in judgment or divine direction. This was especially so when soon after Esther and then Sammy left Guyana for Caribbean Union College in Trinidad. While on one hand it would have been so much easier for them to live at our own home in Trinidad, on the other hand they would have been robbed of the dormitory experience. In addition Sammy might not have been able to make his mark as he did with the children's choir, concerts, and drama at CUC, and leave positive impressions on so many young minds. After her two years Esther completed her program and graduated as valedictorian of her class.

Now ponder this with me. On that morning of the session, I had planned that after breakfast in the cafeteria, while we were in the privacy of our room, I would tell Gordon that if he was nominated, he should let his name go through, and leave it to the Lord to direct the outcome. But I was delayed between the dining hall and our room, and when I arrived he had already left! He was a member of the nominating committee and had left early.

So what do you think? Was the decision to withdraw his name a right or a wrong one? In our musings we have always concluded that it was divine direction, and we have been at peace with that decision. Moreover, when we look back on what was accomplished during those six years, which was one of the most challenging periods of our country's history, and recognize the value of the foundations that were laid in those formative years of the Guyana Conference, we believe that the two term tenure in our homeland was the will of God.

God's Protection

Those years were not only memorable but also eventful. One Sabbath morning Gordon was away, and we were all ready to go to church. Sammy was the first to go down to the car, and he soon came bouncing back up the stairs to breathlessly tell us that the car was jacked up and had no wheels! During the night thieves had scaled the heavily chained gate, stolen all four wheels, and left stacked bricks under the car to keep it up. Thank God they did not come into the house as they had done twice before. Previously thieves had entered the house through an open barred widow in broad daylight when we were out and had taken away our serving dishes, cutlery, and other precious items.

In his attempt to straighten the vehicle away from the Demerara River that bordered the road, it tilted on the two left wheels, leaving the other two suspended in the air.

One day we were traveling from Georgetown to Linden by jeep to promote a personal ministries program. Gordon was driving, and in the vehicle were personnel from the division and the union, along with two or three church members, John, and me. The pastors were talking when we came to an "S" bend on the road. Gordon maneuvered the first curve safely and was about to complete the bend when the jeep skidded on the wet road. In his attempt to straighten the vehicle away from the Demerara River that bordered the road, it tilted on the two left wheels, leaving the other two suspended in the air.

It was as if evil angels and good angels were in a fierce battle for our lives. Eventually, after what seemed like an eternity, the jeep righted itself back on all four wheels, and we all breathed a sigh of relief. The vehicle was not damaged, and except for a slight bruise on my right hand, no one else was hurt. I still bear the mark of that injury—a reminder of how once again the Lord thwarted the plans of the devil and saved us from danger. After a prayer of thanksgiving, we were back on our way to meet with the waiting congregation.

As the years rolled by, the difficulties in Guyana escalated. More food items were banned from entering the country. Clean water was limited, and power outages were prevalent. But amidst the hardships of daily living the work of God prospered—just as it did in the time of the early church. It was during a period of persecution that the believers were scattered and went everywhere preaching the gospel. It was then that Phillip went down to Gaza, met the treasurer of Ethiopia, taught him about Jesus, and baptized him. And this official went on his way, rejoicing to take the gospel to Africa.

My Illness

I was still working tirelessly as hospital chaplain when toward the end of the second term I got ill. I visited different doctors and underwent all kinds of tests, but the diagnosis was inconclusive. Finally, the union committee decided that I should seek medical help in the United States. We contacted Aubrey and Joyce, both employees at Florida Hospital, and they made all the arrangements for me to meet a physician there. So off to Orlando, Florida, I went. The next morning I saw the doctor, and in the afternoon he completed his diagnosis. I had surgery and stayed in Orlando for about a month to recuperate.

One Saturday night Joyce and I were talking late into the night when the doorbell rang. Who could it be at that late hour? As we pulled aside the curtains to see who it was a frightening sight confronted us! The branches of all the trees in the yard were draped with toilet paper! Our minds raced as we thought of the Klu Klux Klan! Maybe they wanted the blacks out of this neighborhood! So we woke up Aubrey and called 911. The officer responded promptly and then assured us that it was one of the teenagers' pranks that they do to all new neighbors. This was their way of saying, "Welcome to the neighborhood." The next morning Nigel and Ray had the job of taking down all the toilet paper, which filled about a half dozen large garbage bags. *What a waste!* I thought. In Guyana, quality toilet paper was a luxury!

Our second term of conference leadership was coming to a close, and another session was on the horizon. It seemed that "Gordon would be Guyana Conference president for life," according to his sister Dolly. At the end of the first term he was unanimously re-elected to serve a second, and he would have easily been elected to serve a third term. But as the session drew near, we became certain that we did not want a third triennium. Gordon discussed our decision with the leaders of the Caribbean Union and the Inter-American Division. Providentially the IAD was looking for evangelists and associate ministerial directors to serve the three major language groups in the territory—English, French, and Spanish. Gordon was appointed to fill the slot for the English and was given the option to live in any of the English-speaking countries in the territory. We chose the island of Trinidad.

Chapter 25

In the Land of the Hummingbird

It was with mixed emotions that we packed our belongings piece by piece. Then in late 1986 we said "goodbye" to our dear Guyana, land of many waters, land of mighty men and maidens, land of our birth. We were about to begin another phase, another chapter of our "exciting life," as Gordon would often say with a big grin on his face and a twinkle in his eye. And to Trinidad we went, land of the Pitch Lake, land of the hummingbird. Do you know that this tiny bird is the only bird that can fly forward and backward and can stay stationary in the air by flapping its wings fifty times per second? It is one of the marvels of God's creation.

When we moved to Trinidad, John was still living with us and was in high school, Sammy was a music education major at Atlantic Union College, and Esther was a chemistry major at Andrews University. Because of the currency restrictions in Guyana, it was difficult to support them financially. They were on their own and were relying on subsidized government grants and loans by working at various jobs on campus. Esther was fortunate to be able to cut costs by staying with her aunt and uncle, Lynette and Kenneth Riley, who lived not far from Andrews. The memory of their financial challenges makes me emotional at times, but once again we were grateful for children who were not afraid to work diligently and yet maintain a good GPA. And again we thank God for His blessings.

In Trinidad we found a lovely house in Avondale Gardens in Maracas not far from the college. In the spacious yard were four Julie mango trees that bore sweet juicy mangoes profusely during the summer months. We had so many mangoes that we would take bags of them to the CUC campus. I have discovered that our God rewards faithfulness in many ways. One retired president looked at me and exclaimed, "Indeed, 'godliness with contentment is great gain.'" I think he wanted to say that in spite of our challenges in Guyana and our sacrifice to return, we both were looking good. God had blessed us, and He was rewarding us.

Getting My Bachelor's Degree

One of the tangible ways that God blessed us was enabling me to complete my first degree. I had left the United States before I could achieve this goal, but now I was able to take advantage of a new church policy that provided tuition for the wives of pastors to complete their baccalaureate degree. At that time CUC was an affiliate of Andrews University, so while I had the convenience of completing my degree locally, I was receiving a degree from a U.S. university! And I finished it free of charge! Isn't God wonderful?

During that summer and the first quarter of the new school year, I had the opportunity to serve as the acting dean of women! I was walking in the footsteps of my eldest sister, Cynthia. Though it was for a short time, I took time to listen to some of the frustrations of the women in my attempt to find ways to get these young ladies to attend morning worship, which was a requirement in those days. Attendance at evening worship was better, and in those sessions I talked to them like a mother to her daughters.

Some of those girls really tried my patience. Just recently on one of our trips I met one of them. After our presentation she came and gave me a big hug. Of course, she had to remind me of who she was and we laughingly recalled the days in the dorm. She updated me on her status and introduced me to her two teenage boys. I was glad to hear that both she and the boys were active in church. On second thought she was in the "bud of womanhood"—that transitional phase called adolescence, which many parents do not comprehend, and I myself did not at the time. She and the other teenagers were growing up, making friends, grappling with those raging hormones, as well as trying to discover themselves by asking identity questions. I was glad for the experience but relieved when they found a permanent dean.

"When God calls a man He bids him come and die." This meant a death to self, a "not my will but Thine be done." And this became my mantra for the days and years ahead.

Of all the classes I took, one religion class stands out in my memory. One of our assignments was to read the book *The Cost of Discipleship* by Dietrich Bohoeffer. It was the opening sentence of the first chapter that impacted my mind for years. It read, "When God calls a man He bids him come and die." This meant a death to self, a "not my will but Thine be done." And this became my mantra for the days and years ahead. Another assignment was to prepare several sermon outlines, develop one of them, then present it to a congregation. I conducted a Wednesday night service at the church in the Maracas Valley not far from where we lived. Those who attended wanted me to return, but I could not make such a promise.

Chapter 25 In the Land of the Hummingbird

Two years later I graduated with a bachelor's degree in elementary education from Andrews University, and soon after I began working as an instructor in the teacher training program at the college. I taught Principles of Teaching and Methods of Teaching, and I arranged for and evaluated the students in their practice teaching. I also had the opportunity to grade the final examination papers of teacher trainees for the government of Trinidad and Tobago in those two areas. At last we were settled and content in our individual roles, Gordon as an evangelist and associate ministerial director of the division and I as an instructor at the college.

After five productive years conducting campaigns in the English territories, during which he experimented with, developed, and refined Family Life Evangelism, at the union session in 1991, Gordon was elected president of the Caribbean Union. The time had now come him for him to assume the leadership that he had turned down nine years before.

Getting My Master's Degree

As I continued instructing at the college, I sensed the need for graduate studies. I contacted an old friend who previously worked with Gordon and was then a professor at Wayne State University in Michigan. We learned that he had helped others in their quest for graduate degrees, and I sent him the required documents. While in the process of making arrangements for me, he discovered that the Inter-American Division had provision for scholarships for college faculty. So I submitted an application through the college president, Dr. Sylvan Lashley, and it was approved. Gordon and I agreed that I would move to Michigan while he and John remained in Trinidad.

So in January 1992, in the middle of winter, I was walking the campus of Andrews University determined to complete the program in as short a time as possible. A two-bedroom university apartment was my home during my stay in Michigan. Although far from home, I was now nearer to my other two children. Esther was working at a pharmaceutical company in Kalamazoo and preparing to do graduate studies at UCLA, and Sammy had recently started teaching at South Lancaster Academy near Atlantic Union College.

By God's grace I completed the graduate program in education with emphasis on curriculum in one year, a feat I would not encourage anyone to dare. We had left the United States with the concern that we were doing so without my achieving my degrees, but now, years later, I had received a master's degree free of charge! So in early January I was back at CUC, anxious to continue where I had left off. Now I would be fully employed and ready to serve my alma mater. But there was another test coming!

According to government regulations, any full-time non-national wanting to work in Trinidad had to apply for a permit. Even though the college serviced other Caribbean islands and was neither owned nor at that time financially subsidized by the Trinidad government, it still had to get this work permit for its "foreign" faculty or staff members. The college applied for mine, and I waited patiently. However, my anxiety level rose when the weeks turned to months without any permit. I do not recall how long it took, but I do recall that at times I became very frustrated. And when the devil tried to fill my mind with negative thoughts, I would drown them out by remembering the lyrics of the hymn "Master, the Tempest Is Raging" by Mary Baker (1874).

This song portrayed the experience of the disciples on that stormy night on the Sea of Galilee. As I sang, I would visualize them battling the huge waves, crying out to Jesus who was sleeping in the boat. The words are as follows:

> Master, the tempest is raging!
>
> The billows are tossing high!
>
> The sky is o'ershadowed with blackness,
>
> No shelter or help is nigh;
>
> "Carest Thou not that I perish?"
>
> How canst Thou lie asleep,
>
> When each moment so madly is threat'ning
>
> A grave in the angry deep?

Then I would imagine Jesus getting up amidst the roar of the wind and the tossing of the boat. I could see Him calmly lifting His hand and saying, "Peace, be still!" The sea lies at rest and the disciples watch in wonder. Then I would feel a little better and continue to sing the chorus:

> The winds and the waves shall obey Thy will,
>
> Peace, be still! Peace, be still!
>
> Whether the wrath of the storm-tossed sea,
>
> Or demons, or men, or whatever it be,
>
> No water can swallow the ship where lies
>
> The Master of ocean and earth and skies;
>
> They all shall sweetly obey Thy will;
>
> Peace! Peace! be still!

Sometimes by the end of the chorus peace would flood my own soul. But at other times I had to sing the second stanza:

> Master, with anguish of spirit
>
> I bow in my grief today;
>
> The depths of my sad heart are troubled;
>
> Oh, waken and save, I pray;
>
> Torrents of sin and of anguish
>
> Sweep o'er my sinking soul;
>
> And I perish! I perish! dear Master;
>
> Oh, hasten, and take control"

Again peace would flood my soul at which time I would sing the chorus as well as the last stanza:

> Master the terror is over,
>
> The elements sweetly rest;
>
> Earth's sun in the calm lake is mirrored,
>
> And heaven's within my breast;
>
> Linger, O blessed Redeemer!
>
> Leave me alone no more
>
> And with joy I shall make the blest harbor,
>
> And rest on the blissful shore.

At one time the frustration was so overwhelming that I cried out, "God, is this what I get for being a faithful minister's wife? As far as I know I have tried to do what You wanted me to do and go where You wanted me to go." Once again I was complaining!

Then one day the permit arrived! And I was able to join the faculty at CUC, instructing in both the two-year teacher training program and the four-year college courses. I taught Psychology of Education, Sociology of Education, Instructional Media, and Classroom Management, and I volunteered to teach Psychology of Exceptional Children when they were in dire need of a teacher. For my extracurricular activity I advised the Education Club and planned an education day with the student leaders. The theme was "Paint the World with Love," and I was chosen to be the speaker. So I preached at CUC!

I was settling in at my alma mater, hoping to do what I could to motivate students to excellence, help them achieve their goals, and challenge them to be of service wherever their loving Father would lead. What a joy it was for me to teach and impart knowledge to others! And I began to look forward to working on the doctoral program with the assurance that my Friend would provide as He always did.

Don't Scare Me, Johnny!

John was still with us and was able to enjoy the comforts of a lovely home while completing high school and then college at CUC. One night he gave us a scare. It was almost midnight and he was not home! Since we lived so near the school, he would often walk home. He definitely could not be at the library or with his friends on a school night. So Gordon and I got in the car, and with my imagination running wild and the window down, I kept shouting his name, "Johnny! Johnny!" No answer. In frustration, we finally gave up, returned home, and prayed for his safety, asking God to prepare us for whatever fate might come that night. We were thankful to God when he finally appeared. He had walked home with a friend, who on the way was laying all her grievances at his feet, and he had accompanied her to her home. Those were the days before cell phones!

Talking of scares, Johnny was noted for causing us anxiety. It happened when we were returning to Guyana in 1977. He was five. As mentioned before, en route we were state hopping to visit relatives, and we stopped in Maryland to spend a few days with Aubrey and his family. On the way to their home, we entered a shopping plaza to make a purchase. It was nighttime, and the stores were decorated with hundreds of blinking lights. Christmas was in the air! My brother knew where to go, and we all followed him into the store while the children wandered off to feast their eyes on the toys that screamed, "Buy me! Buy me!"

When the purchase was completed, we called the children and all piled into the car. All, except John! Unnoticed, he had slipped away from the rest, had wandered into another section of the store, and did not hear the round up call. On the way home, my maternal instincts kicked in and I said, "Joyce, is Johnny there with you in the front?"

"No, isn't he in the back?"

"No!"

In the crowded car we had taken it for granted that all the children were in. Fear gripped my heart! How could we find him in all the hustle and bustle of Christmas shoppers here, there, and everywhere? And it was night!

In the crowded car we had taken it for granted that all the children were in. Fear gripped my heart! How could we find him in all the hustle and bustle of Christmas shoppers here, there, and everywhere?

So we prayed, turned around, and headed back to the store. When I jumped out of the car and ran in, there he was with tears in his eyes and an officer beside him. Relieved and very happy, I hugged him tight and thanked the officer. Finally, all the children were in! Parents need to ask the question daily, "Are all the children in? The night is falling!" Somehow I could not spank him nor fret with him. All that mattered was that my son was safe in my arms. We thanked God for his safe keeping.

In the same way, God rejoices over His children when they are found. Isn't that what Jesus taught in the three parables of the lost coin, the lost sheep, and lost son recorded in Luke 15? When the woman found her lost coin she rejoiced, and when the shepherd found his lost sheep he rejoiced. And when the lost son who was tempted and enticed finally came to his senses, made up his mind, and trudged back home, he fell into loving arms of the waiting Father who night by night had been watching for him. At that memorable moment when the Father saw his bedraggled son in the distance, he ran, hugged him, kissed him, robed him, welcomed him, and threw the biggest welcome home party, inviting all to rejoice with Him. Our loving heavenly Father continues to wait, watching and peering into the darkness for each of His lost children to come home. Let Him throw a welcome home party for you.

After John graduated from CUC, he moved to New York to continue his studies while he worked. He completed training as an X-ray tech at Hostos College, and this provided him with a handsome income. In retrospect, I think that this was a move for which he was not yet ready. Facing life in the "Big Apple" could be very challenging. However, he did well academically and graduated from New York University with a bachelor's degree in economics.

What's Next?

In addition to my teaching load, I was asked to be shepherdess co-director of the Caribbean Union and work closely with the wife of the union ministerial secretary. However, because of a severe illness to which she later succumbed, she could not function adequately. This organization is designed to nurture the spouses of pastors, and our vision was to have shepherdess leaders in every conference and mission in the union. Under God that goal was gradually achieved. We prepared a Union Shepherdess Bulletin and arranged for a group of shepherdesses to render special music at one of the ordination services.

At the end of the 1995 school year, the chair of the Department of Education left for permanent residence in the United States, and I was appointed acting chair of the department. But before I could assume my new responsibility, another change came! In the summer of that year the General Conference session of the world church convened in Holland, and Gordon was elected vice president of Inter-American Division of the General Conference. That required us to move to the division's headquarters in Miami.

You could imagine that I left the college with mixed emotions. One good thing was that I did not have to think about renewal of my work permit. As usual I was ready to stand at any door of opportunity that my loving Friend might open for me. As the saying goes, "When God closes a window, He opens a door." And I tell you, it was a door bigger than I could ever have dreamed of! I could never have imagined the excitement I would experience in the broader area of service that awaited both of us at the IAD headquarters.

Part Five:
Ministry at the Inter-American Division

Chapter 26

Organizing a Brand New Department

Coming Full Circle!

It is sometimes said, "What goes around comes around" and makes a full circle. This was our experience. We had left the United States eighteen years before, uncertain of ever returning. But now, in God's own time, we were returning! We were coming to live and work from Miami. After the GC session in Holland we went back to Trinidad and began the arduous task of selling and packing our belongings. Unfortunately, Mom was not alive to welcome us to the United States with her favorite tune, "Oh, you weary travelers!"

Since Gordon had made a prior commitment to conduct an evangelistic campaign in Arima, Trinidad, I took on the job of boxing books, our treasured items, selling what could be sold, trashing what could be trashed, and attending the program. After four weeks, the last sermon was preached in Arima, the last person was buried in the watery grave of baptism, acknowledgements and fond farewells were made, and the day came when we finally said goodbye to Trinidad and headed for Miami!

This meant no more annual trips to the States to fulfill requirements for residence status. No more apprehension as we passed through immigration! No more efforts to be economical with the truth as we were questioned about our length of stay abroad. I well remember Sammy being with us when he was returning after being at CUC for more than a year. The Hispanic officer drilled us relentlessly!

He asked me to show him my driver's license, and I told him I didn't have one. I was glad that I really did not have my Guyana license with me. He sent Sammy to a room for further questioning. Gordon went with him while I waited, praying for a positive outcome. Fortunately, the officer they met was more understanding when he was told that Sammy was a student at CUC. We all breathed a sigh of relief when he finally stamped the passport. Now we thanked God that all that was behind us! A new life lay ahead!

Gordon's work was assured, for he was vice president of the division. But here I was with a graduate degree and no job! I had also done a crash course in order to be computer literate. Actually, it was a good thing that I was not employed immediately, for it gave us time to look for and purchase a house, which we found at 14501 SW 137 Court. I then set about unpacking and furnishing our new home.

But when all of that was done, the question was, "What do I do now?" The Adventist high school needed an English teacher, but I was not qualified for the position, so I perused the daily papers in search of work, but my quest was futile. While I waited I was asked to do odd jobs at the division office, especially assisting Georgina, secretary to the president. Somehow it was difficult for me to get into the routine of being a secretary. In Trinidad I had a secretary! I remember one day when the president's secretary was on vacation, and I was left to perform her tasks. I was typing a letter when the current dipped and the computer went off. I was definitely frustrated and the president saw it and helped me retrieve the document. Then there was the mail that I should have sorted and taken to his office. Even when he asked, "Is that the mail?" All I said was "Yes," but I left it right there! I didn't know my daily secretarial duty. I guess that later he picked it up and took it to his office himself.

First IAD Women's Ministries Director

What happened next was quite unexpected. Women's Ministries was a new department of the church, with a director already at the General Conference, but none at our division. To my surprise, I was asked to be the director for the Inter-American Division! I knew a little about shepherdess, but nothing about women's ministries! In fact, I had not even heard about such a ministry before.

Strange as this new ministry was to me, I knew that my Friend would help me. As usual, I had my talk with Him in my private devotions as well as our family worship. But sensing my need, I included a talk with Him when I arrived at my office each morning. I would kneel at my desk to seek wisdom and direction to make the ministry acceptable to Him and to bring Him glory. More prayer, more power! There were many hurdles, some high and some not so high. The first one was to convince the union presidents to accept a ministry where women would lead out—something that was anathema, especially in the "macho minded" Spanish culture.

I have to tip my hat to Pastor Israel Leito, the division president, for being a proactive leader. He arranged for a leadership summit for administrative and departmental planning. There he asked me to give a brief introduction of the ministry to the union presidents and then meet with the prospective women's ministries directors of the various unions in their own group. He advised me to emphasize the philosophy, which is a quote from *Welfare Ministry*. It reads, "The Lord has a work for women as well as for men. They may take their places in His work at this crisis, and He will work through them.... They can do in families a work that men cannot do, a work that reaches the inner life. They can come close to the hearts of those whom men cannot reach. Their labor is needed" (White, p. 145).

The truth is at that meeting some of the presidents were so anti-women's ministries that it became chaotic. In the end most of them left with a huff and a puff! Nothing much was accomplished with them, so I needed a different strategy. In spite of the negativity, the women's sessions with the women's ministries leaders were more productive. I was surprised to learn that some of them were well acquainted with the ministry. The theme that I was inspired to use was "empowering women for time and eternity." We had a wonderful time discussing and planning for this new ministry in our division.

Not long after the summit, I received my first invitation. The East Jamaican Conference asked me to lead out in their weekend activity. This meant I had to prepare a sermon for Friday night, one for the Sabbath worship service, and a third for Sunday morning devotion. On Sabbath afternoon we had a question and answer period on how to survive the first year of marriage. It was only by the grace of God that I got through that weekend! I was tired but happy. On my return to the office, I took time to evaluate my presentations, especially the sermons, and make necessary adjustments. This was surely a foretaste of what was to come. Was I up to the task? Only time would tell!

Our Strategy

Before launching any major program, you must have a plan. Before you write a paper, young people, you have to have a plan or outline. Before they created man, the Trinity had a plan. So I had to have a plan. My number one priority after the summit was to prepare a strategic plan for the advancement of this new department. It included:

1. Appointment of a women's ministries director in every union of the division. That required that the union presidents be convinced of the validity and credibility of this new ministry.

2. PowerPoint presentation of the philosophy, activities, and growth of the ministry at the mid-year and year-end committee meetings of the IAD where the union presidents were in attendance. After those presentations they felt "safe" with the leadership and direction of the ministry, and the "wall of partition" gradually began to break down and the ministry was slowly accepted.

I was overjoyed when I finally received a call from the newly appointed women's ministries director of the South Mexican Union to have a one-to-one consultation. I rejoiced because that union was the largest in the division but the last to come on board. I spent two days with Erna, introducing her to the ministry, outlining the strategy, and answering all her questions. I discovered that, like me, she was an educator with a graduate degree in education and was the wife of the executive secretary of the union. Like me, she embraced the ministry fully, and under God moved it forward to the extent that eventually I visited every conference in the union even as far as a place called Toluca, one of the highest points in Mexico.

3. Frequent articles for the IAD newsletter. The response to this was overwhelming! Invitations from the fields came one after another.

4. Preparation and presentation of two important seminars that I ensured were included on the program wherever I went.

   a) The first was "The Dynamics of Women's Ministries." This seminar was informed in part by the GC handbook and mostly by inspiration. It introduced all aspects of the ministry—reasons for negative reactions to the ministry, the definition of women's ministries, how it got started, why it exists, philosophy, focus issues, and the special days. It also gave the biblical concepts and the vision and mission statements, which Gordon called "inspired." They are: The Vision, "The life of every woman enriched for time and eternity." The Mission, "To mentor the 'young,' nurture the disadvantaged, challenge the educated, and train all in service of love to others. We envision women who are united by prayer, know the Word, and model graces of Christian womanhood."

   b) The second seminar was "Seven Steps to Begin an Effective Ministry."

   This presentation began with our knowing that we are accepted by God as we accept Him. Learning to accept ourselves frees us to accept others. The other steps included: Pray for guidance. Know the ministry. Form a team including the wife of the pastor (if possible). Work with the pastor. Make plans and formulate reachable goals. Choose the simplest plan. Develop the details. Share the responsibilities. Advertise extensively. Execute the program. Take time to evaluate by answering three questions—what went well, what didn't go so well, how we can improve.

3. Providing materials for the women's ministries special days. I prepared seminars on spiritual gifts, health, family issues as pertaining to women, literacy, small groups, and other evangelistic activities. And as the women grasped the concept and implemented the ideas, the administrators, pastors, and their spouses saw the value of this ministry, and they gave their full support. Directors were appointed not only in all the unions but also in the various conferences.

Chapter 26 Organizing a Brand New Department

The division administrators apparently were pleased with my leadership because by the end of my first year as women's ministries director they added family ministries to my portfolio. Even now as I write this memoir I pause in wonder at the accomplishments of this small five-foot, 104-pound Guyanese woman! And then I thank God for giving me the honor to work with and for Him. King David felt the same way when he mused, "Who am I, O Lord God? And what is my house, that You have brought me this far? And yet this was a small thing in Your sight … O Lord God. What more can David say to You for the honor of Your servant?" (1 Chron. 17:16–18).

If God can use me, He can surely use you! Surrender to Him, my child, surrender to Him. Say and sing from the depths of your heart: "Take my life and let it be, consecrated Lord to Thee."

Chapter 27

"Happy in the Service of the King!"

Many years ago we used a songbook called *Singing Youth*. Those from that era will tell you of the inspiration we received not only from singing the tunes but also from meditating on the words. Some of them reached to the depth of the soul, urging us to respond. Very often they motivated us to place our faith in God and unselfishly serve our fellow human beings. One of them was: I am happy in the service of the King,

> I am happy, oh, so happy;
>
> I have peace and joy that nothing else can bring,
>
> In the service of the King!
>
> In the service of the King,
>
> Every talent I will bring;
>
> I have peace and joy and blessing
>
> In the service of the King.

(A. H. Ackley, "In the Service of the King," 1912).

Over the years I have found that it is a joy to serve the Lord in spite of the challenges we face. And that was especially so for me at IAD. The Inter-American Division services about forty countries extending from Mexico, the whole of Central America, all the islands of the Caribbean, and Columbia, Venezuela, and the Guianas on the top of South America. It currently boasts a membership of over 3.5 million, making it the largest of the thirteen divisions of the General Conference.

The organizational structure of the Adventist Church begins with members who form churches. Churches grouped together form conferences (or missions, if they lack adequate financial or leadership support), conferences form unions, and unions form the divisions of the General Conference. At that time IAD had a membership of about 1.5 million, thirteen unions, and seventy conferences and missions. The three main languages are English, French, and Spanish. The head office is located in Miami, and is the only division with its main office situated outside the territory it services. Some time previously the headquarters was in Cuba. Miami was later chosen because it is the hub for travel to most of the division's territories as well as its stable currency.

Challenges

Every job has its challenges. But sometimes the things we call challenges are only opportunities to greater achievements. One big challenge was dealing with the various languages. Every program we used had to be given to the translators early enough so that it could reach the field on time. These included the three special days for women's ministry—Day of Prayer in March, Women's Ministries Emphasis Day in June, and Abuse Prevention Day in September—as well as the two special days for family ministries in February and September. While it is true that we received some materials from the GC, we still had to make adjustments or rewrite them in order to make them relevant for the fields. Then think of the seminars and sermons the union, conference, and mission directors requested for their weekend retreats. And the theme and seminars requested were different for each event! It was a herculean task!

The other challenge was maintaining travel schedules over such a scattered territory. This required hours waiting at airports, and even missing events because of plane delays and sudden changes in flight schedules. Gordon had his carry-on case that had his computer, Bible, folders of material, and other things stolen at one crowded airport, and I missed a women's ministries weekend activity in St. Vincent. The flight took me through Puerto Rico to connect with the propeller plane, because the runway in St. Vincent was not long enough to allow the landing of larger planes. However, in Puerto Rico the connecting flight was delayed, and after the twin-engine plane with its buzzing propellers arrived, we were told to prepare for boarding. While we waited for the plane to be sanitized, the next announcement we heard was that the flight was canceled because of insufficient daylight at the airport! They provided accommodation for the night, and I arrived at my destination the next afternoon when the program was almost over.

We had a similar problem when Gordon and I were on our way to Guadeloupe for a family ministries leaders' workshop. On that occasion we had to turn back at Puerto Rico and return home because arriving the next day would have been worthless. In those cases we simply said, "God knows best." In some of those situations, I welcomed the rest or used the extra hours to prepare or put the finishing touches on the next scheduled presentation. Our God is good all the time.

Joys and Thrills of Travel

But travel also had its joys, and one of them was the joy of meeting new people and seeing new places. This ministry took me to every corner of the division's territory and even to places where the administrators had not gone. I traveled in the Boeing 727 and 737, as well as in the comfort of the large 747 or jumbo jets, and once on the 777. Almost all the time I traveled in coach, but occasionally I was upgraded to business class and even first class. And while I enjoyed the ride, I marveled at the wisdom our God has given man to keep that mass of material in the air. Several times I traveled in propeller planes and the small single-engine ones where you can see all the controls and even touch the pilot. I knew which cloud formations would trigger a bumpy ride, and I knew the sounds the planes made on takeoff, on descent, and on landing.

Once we had just taken off from Miami en route to Puerto Rico when I heard a strange grating sound and knew something was wrong. But there was no word from the pilot. My discomfort level rose a notch higher when I heard that sound again. Those who travel will agree that it is comforting when the pilot speaks. Then the pilot told us that the flap on the landing gear was not receding as it should. He said that we could continue the flight but it would be slow going, and so he had decided to return to the airport. He quickly added that he could not land immediately but had to circle a few times to let out some of the fuel from the engine.

On the descent the pilot warned that fire could erupt from the landing gear grating against each other. When we finally touched down at the airport, fire trucks and ambulances were in place in case of emergency. We all breathed a sigh of relief and thanked the pilot for a safe landing. And so I sing my version of Edward Hopper's hymn "Jesus, Savior, Pilot Me":

Jesus, Saviour, pilot me

[In the air and on the sea.]

[Grating gears around me roll,]

Hiding rock and treacherous shoal;

Chart and compass come from thee,

Jesus, Saviour, pilot me. (1871)

Sometimes it was smooth sailing in clear sunny skies, and other times it was bumpy amid dark clouds. Often the pilot would alert us about the weather ahead. In fact, one pilot went so far as to reassure us that during turbulence they know what to do. On another trip between Miami and Costa Rica, the voice we heard was that of a female pilot. It was my first experience flying with one of my own gender. I learned from her that the pilot does not release the landing gear until she or he sees the runway. She also alerted us to the fact that it was difficult to see the runway in Costa Rica when it was cloudy. This meant that she would have to prepare to land and hopefully succeed, and if not she would have to return to the flying position and try landing again or defer to another airport. Thank God, she saw the runway.

Would you believe it when I tell you that in my early days I was afraid to fly? In some of my early trips abroad, Gordon would hold my hands on takeoff. Of course, my fear was not as bad as that of my sister Ruby who once, after her plane was in the air, called for the flight attendant and told her that she wanted to get off the plane! I was often told that flying in the sky was safer than driving in a car on land, but if anything should happen in the sky, there was nothing a person could do about it but follow the instructions and hope for the best. My comfort was that my "Father up above was always looking down in love." One reassuring text to remember reads: "The eternal God is Your Refuge and underneath are the everlasting arms" (Deut. 33:27). *The Clear Word* puts this same verse as follows: "His everlasting arms will hold you up forever."

Then there was travel on sea in big boats and small boats like the catamaran in which the women's ministries directors of the Caribbean Union and Grenada Mission and I traveled in from Grenada to Carriacou. We set sail in gorgeous weather. The sea was so calm that we took seats on the open deck of the boat with the wind in our hair and the kiss of the warm sunshine on our cheeks. But not long after dark clouds appeared in the sky, fierce winds began to blow, and coupled with the rain, the sea was churned into huge waves. That catamaran heaved high and low as it rode the waves and battled the stormy weather. Somehow I did not get sick as my two colleagues and others in the boat did. After about two hours, which seemed like an eternity, we finally reached land and were glad to arrive at our destination. What a journey it must have been for the apostle Paul to spend fourteen days on the open tempestuous sea on his way to Italy (Acts 27)!

On land I traveled in good cars and very old cars that broke down on the way. I stayed in top quality hotels and some low quality ones. At times I lodged in homes, and other times at camps without hot water. I mingled with all kinds of people—the learned and the eager to learn. And I stopped to talk with the curious children and answer their questions like, "What is your real name?" or "When you were a child, did you ever fight?"

Often I was treated like a celebrity. People lined up wanting to take a picture with me, have me write in their hymnbooks, Bibles, or even on a small scrap of paper, or have me pray with them. Some would even purchase Bibles or hymnals on the spot so I could autograph it and write a message. I conducted several radio interviews and a couple television interviews in the Bahamas and Puerto Rico. I received all kinds of precious gifts—some handcrafted and beautiful, and others not so much—but I accepted them all as coming from grateful hearts. At times I was able to visit the tourist attractions, eat and enjoy a variety of foods, and learn a bit of the culture, which caused me to appreciate and love the people more. It is reassuring to know that "the Lord will record, when He registers the peoples: 'This one was born there'" (Ps. 87:6).

Both Gordon and I also had the joy of traveling to places outside the division territory. After the General Conference session in Holland, we were able to tour parts of Europe with the rest of the Caribbean delegation. We went to Italy, Germany, Rome and the Vatican, France, and Switzerland where we were able to connect with Esther who was studying there at the time.

We were privileged to walk in the footsteps of the apostle Paul and visit the places he worked. We started in Turkey and visited Corinth, Athens, and Ephesus. We sat on the steps of the open-air theatre where the clerk quieted the riotous crowd that kept on shouting, "Great is Diana of the Ephesians!" The acoustics were simply amazing! They had no sound system, no powerful microphones, but you could sit anywhere in that extensive stadium, even to the far back, and clearly hear what the speaker in the front was saying. We sat to the back of the theatre and heard the song sung by our quartet as loudly and clearly as if we were up front. I dare to call it a technological marvel at that time. Then we crossed the blue waters of the Mediterranean and traveled to Patmos where the apostle John was imprisoned, had his visions, and penned book of Revelation. It was an experience I will always remember and treasure!

Countries With Great Challenges

There is the thrill of travel and there is the joy of sharing. As the ditty says, "I have two pencils and I am glad; You have no pencils, and that's too bad! I'll share my pencils for I love you, And now you have a nice pencil too."

Ministry I daresay lends itself to experience the joy of sharing in a variety of ways. Under God I shared spiritual blessings through sermons and seminars, as well as material blessings with those in need. In those challenging days in Cuba, people lacked everyday necessities—bath soap, oil, mosquito nets, and shoes for their children. Every year I took at least two suitcases with specific items for those who asked and good clothing for those who needed. The amazing thing was that I was never asked to open any of my suitcases when I passed through customs at the airport.

The more I mingled with the Cuban people the more I marveled at their ingenuity. They excelled in music and arts and crafts—they made ornaments from simple things. I have in my collection crafts made from whole dried coconut. As for the chauffeurs, they were exceptional! They are able to keep their fifty-year-old cars running. And if a problem arose, they fixed it themselves, or walked the distance to get the necessary help. They always got us to our destination! I am sure there was a convoy of holy angels with us to ward off the bad ones, for we infrequently had car problems. "Bless the Lord, O my soul, and forget not all thy benefits" (Ps. 103:2).

The other country with grave challenges was Haiti. But they were different. They never asked for anything even though I prompted a request! Even from the skies, one could sense the dense poverty that existed. Before landing you couldn't escape seeing the burnt out forest areas. Internal air travel was quite scary because of the age of the planes. You boarded the plane with a prayer on your lips for safety and one of thanksgiving upon safe arrival. Road travel was just as bad or even worse.

On one occasion, Gordon and I traveled from the capital city of Port-au-Prince to Gonaives, a town that had experienced terrible floods that had resulted in much loss of life and destruction of property. Along the way the car tire gave out two times, but there was only one spare! We waited for hours, hungry, dusty, and tired, and we breathed a sigh of relief when help finally arrived. The people work hard, and the children look out and care for one another. And on Sabbath mornings the churches are packed to capacity! Some churches conduct two services, and you had to be early to find a seat at the 8:00 a.m. service! One Sabbath the union president took me to preach at the university church. We marveled at the pride of the people, their faith in their God, and their dedication to His work. The faithful will surely have their reward.

Although some of the countries caused heart throbbing fear, somehow I was never afraid to stay alone in my hotel room. In the nights when I secured the door and said a prayer to my Friend, I always slept like a baby. The leaders were always careful to choose the best and safest hotel in the area. The leaders also worked us to the bone during our visit. On the evening of arrival, having traveled all day, they expected you to preach or make a presentation to the excited and waiting audience that often packed the venue to capacity.

On the other side of sharing is the joy of receiving. For the paradox is true: It is in giving that you receive. God helped me in the preparation of seminars in different ways. Sometimes He directed me to find books that dealt with the specific topic I was asked to address. Once He helped me put together a presentation while I was high up in the sky! I had struggled with the topic for a while and just could not get it together. I was able to complete it during the flight, and it turned out to be one of the best. I received inspiration to carry on as I saw how creative and talented the women were in the planning and execution of their programs. And many of their themes were out of this world! Usually the events were held at special venues where the women attended in huge numbers.

Only once did I experience opposition. A dear brother used Scripture to angrily oppose what was said, but he did not have the courage to wait for me to respond with quotes from the Bible as well. He left after delivering his scathing remarks. In many of the Hispanic countries, some husbands accompanied their wives, and when they liked what they heard, they wanted to take pictures with me and their family. This was a good thing because it made them realize that the ministry was not preaching women's liberation or ordination, but it was encouraging overall improvement of each woman in her spiritual journey. It is a fact that when the status of the woman improves the entire family is enriched.

Chapter 28

Educator and Evangelist

Sermons and Seminars

As the women's ministries director, I had to preach sermons that were relevant to women. Although I had no formal training in this area, Gordon had introduced me to preaching years ago, and of course I had heard dozens of his sermons over three decades. Above all was the inspiration of God's Holy Spirit. Some of my sermons were: "Woman with a Vision of her Mission," a message on Esther; "Up! For this is the day!" a sermon on Deborah; "Who Dialed 911?" on Lydia and the demon possessed slave, and "Four Strategies for Success," a sermon on Joshua and many more.

I did a lot of preaching and also a lot of teaching. My background in education was a valuable asset in the preparation of specific seminars I was asked to present. Some of the seminar topics were living with a non-SDA spouse, singleness, communication, motherhood, coping with divorce, what to do with a cheating spouse, married again and with children, domestic violence, the efficacy of prayer, how to improve one's devotional life, and many more. The majority of them were PowerPoint presentations.

Little did I realize the prevalence of domestic violence until I was asked to present a seminar on this subject in Medellin, Colombia. Even though there was prayer meeting in the sanctuary above, the people crowded in the room below to hear the presentation. They asked questions and told of seeking help from pastors who often suggested that they conform

Chapter 28 Educator and Evangelist

to the duty of the Christian wife and stay "until death do them part." We cannot be too quick to condemn the pastors because at that time they did not know about this monster and they gave the best counsel they knew. I later came to realize that the majority of the seminars they requested were the felt needs of the women. My belief was confirmed when I received various notes from the women after a domestic violence presentation. One of them read, "All that you said is true. I have been in an abusive relationship for eighteen years, and I cannot get out!"

The next place where this seminar was presented was at a campsite in Mexico. When the leaders sent the invitation, they did not request any specific seminar, neither did they inform me that this was a joint event with the personal ministries leaders. I was reluctant to present that topic because I was unsure of how the men would react. I "racked my brain" and prayerfully tried to find something more suitable for that mixed group, but somehow I could not come up with another topic. So with some reservation I presented the domestic violence topic in Spanish, aided by PowerPoint.

As I proceeded I was relieved to discover that what I said resonated with both the men and women. As they listened, they added their comments, even relating a recent incident of a spouse who lost her life as a result of domestic violence. The dear mother did not know what to do so she stayed in the relationship and suffered the consequences. At present, much to the relief of many, this monster is being publicly addressed by many organizations in the United States and by a few family ministries directors in their churches.

At the end of the seminar that morning, women and men at that campsite spontaneously stood in a round of applause, which went on for at least two minutes! When I realized that they would not stop, I invited first the union and then the conference women's ministries directors to the platform to take a bow with me. It was simply amazing! I do not know how many persons were in that situation and needed that information that day but I silently offered a prayer of thanks to my Father and Friend for compelling me to present that seminar.

The two other times I received sustained applause were in the Bahamas after presenting a seminar they requested titled "Friendships of Women" and at the Mt. Olive Church after preaching the Mother's Day sermon titled "What Makes a Mother After All?" On another occasion, although there was not applause after presenting the topic "The Million Dollar Question," a retired minister came to me and said he had to shake my hand for that sermon. Thank you, Gordon, for teaching me how to speak. And thank God for women's ministries that gave women a forum to address their needs and improve the quality of their lives.

By the way, I am writing these things not to boast, but to encourage. It is to assure each reader that if God can use me, He can use you to do great things for Him. To my dear children, I say, surrender to Him. Let Him lead you, John, with your musical, creative, intelligent mind, computer skills, and other talents; let Him lead you, Sammy, your intelligent mind, musical, leadership, and entertaining abilities; and let Him lead you, Esther and Marco, with your brilliant analytical minds, leadership skills, and musical and technological abilities. Surrender to Him, my dear reader, whoever you are.

Evangelistic Campaigns

Not only did I teach through seminars, I also conducted several evangelistic campaigns. My first series was held in Nicaragua, and it was a real marathon. During the day I had to finish preparing the sermon, sort out the graphics for the overhead projector, and then preach to a packed audience at night. Believe it or not, I spoke every night for two weeks to keep the momentum going and twice on the two Sabbaths! As if that was not enough, I had to keep the appointments they had arranged for me. One of these was a visit to the prison where they had an active ministry. That was a moving experience!

That campaign was followed by other evangelistic programs in Cuba and different parts in Columbia. There was a one-week revival in Medellin. Then two campaigns in Cucuta where about half a dozen couples living together were married and baptized. In Bucaramanga the campaign was conducted in a city church that had a large congregation with lots of professionals, and it was situated in the heart of a dominant Catholic community. Every night the church was filled with members and visitors, and I expected a good response. Much to my dismay, on the night I made the call, no one came forward! As I continued to call, the Lord moved on the heart of a little girl, and when she came forward the adults followed. Indeed "a little child shall lead them."

> *As I continued to call, the Lord moved on the heart of a little girl, and when she came forward the adults followed. Indeed "a little child shall lead them."*

At the close of the meeting that night, when most of the people had left for home, a lady from the community walked up the aisle to talk with me. In her halting English she expressed appreciation for the nightly presentations, adding, "The truth is in the messages you present!" Then she signed the card for baptism that my attendant gave her. The pastor of the church was ecstatic! He just could not believe what he was seeing. That night in every waking moment I prayed that our God will help her stand by her decision. On Sabbath morning we looked for her, but had to come to the sad conclusion that her conviction did not translate into action. Later I learned she was a devout Catholic, a woman of means and an icon in her community. I do hope that she later had the courage to put pride aside and follow Jesus all the way.

When a couple in Giron who had been living together for years decided to get married and be baptized, the members rallied to the occasion and did what they could to make it a memorable experience for the couple. I did the sermonette for the wedding, and later was asked by the ministerial secretary to address the pastors. I should have declined the request at such a short invitation but was glad that I accepted it. God rewarded my efforts and those of the women who worked tirelessly to prepare the fields and fill the churches in those eight evangelistic campaigns, which resulted in the baptism of about four hundred converts.

As family ministries director I had to prepare sermons and seminars for the two annual special days in February and September. I was invited to family retreats where I preached and presented seminars on requested topics. Some of these meetings were for pastoral families, and at one of these events I was surprised to discover that one of these leaders could find nothing for which to affirm his spouse even

Chapter 28 Educator and Evangelist

though he had been married for many years! Could it be that there was trouble in pastoral families as well?

In order to better acquaint myself with the intricacies of the family, I registered for summer classes at Andrews University to become a certified family life educator. I finished all the requirements and completed the assignments, but unfortunately, before printing the documents my old computer crashed. It was work done but labor lost, and that gave me a sinking feeling in the pit of my stomach. But there was nothing I could have done since those were not the days of thumb drives and backups. So I do not have the certificate of completion. However, I attended the GC Family Councils, studied the manual and other materials they provided, and read several books in a variety of topics. Yes, it was challenging to lead out in those two ministries, but there is joy in service.

So there I was! Instead of walking the cloistered halls of academia, I was out in the vineyard, plowing, sowing, harvesting, and crushing grapes to produce juice. The Lord blessed and guided both the Women's Ministries and Family Ministries Departments, and the results were amazing. For me, His promise held true, "I will instruct you and teach you in the way you should go; I will guide you with My eye" (Ps. 32:8).

Meet My Special Helpers!

My first special helper was Dhalia, a fearless warrior of the cross and an inspiration to me. As women's ministries director of Nicaragua, she injected the women with the vaccines of positive self-esteem and evangelistic fervor at a prayer breakfast. She and her husband, President Miguel, trained them, gave them sermon booklets, and challenged them to find places to conduct their evangelistic meetings. When I visited the mission, there were women preaching everywhere with attendance ranging from about ten to twenty. And men were listening to the women and responding to their appeals!

At the close, Ardis Stenbakken, the General Conference women's ministries director, and I gathered at the river with pastors and church members to witness the baptism of over nine hundred converts, which at that time, was the largest in the history of the Nicaragua Mission! To God be the glory! She not only inspired me, but she also began to arrange for my campaign. However, she and her husband were transferred to another field and could not be present when I made my debut in evangelism. Thanks, Dhalia!

In Bucharamanga and Giron, I met Dr. Tatiana and her husband, Carlos. She was my translator, fluent in both Spanish and English, and he was our chauffeur. As we worked together, our friendship grew as we shared common interests, sometimes stopped for ice cream, and did other fun things together. This lovely couple later became the parents of two beautiful children—a boy and a girl. Our friendship continues to this day through social media, and two of their family pictures are used in our Happy Family television episodes.

Then there was Joel. He was a young pastor who worked closely with me in Cucuta, Colombia. When I met him he was single, and he often shared with me his frustration over the attempts of his well-meaning family to find a wife for him. Once they arranged for him to meet someone of their liking and got very upset with him when he denied their choice. He confided, "I just did not like her." Since then, he has found someone he loves and is married and has a daughter. He still calls me occasionally to update me on his married life and to tell of his challenges with his churches. He calls me his "mom from afar." Recently he called excitedly to tell me that his daughter will have a brother. So I now have two Columbian "grandchildren from afar!"

One of my very special helpers was Maribel whose parents were Jamaican immigrants to Cuba. She was bilingual and a graduate of the Cuban University, but she was unemployed because of her religious beliefs. When I met her, she was working part time at the conference and was assigned to be my translator. She traveled with me everywhere, and at the end the director asked that I reimburse her for her services. I gladly gave to the director what she suggested, and she in turn paid Maribel. I really do not know what happened, but on my return the next year she had been relieved of her work at the office. This affected her greatly so that she had lost weight and was not flashing her usual winsome smile.

I used the only weapon we had and took it the Lord in prayer. After days of uplifting her before the throne of grace in my personal devotions, I felt impressed to try to get her to CUC, our college in Trinidad. It seemed like a crazy idea, but I believed that if that was God's plan for her, He would see it through. And our loving Father honored our faith. As she updated me on her progress, it seemed to me that every step she made, every government office she visited, He was right beside her to make it possible. With all the relevant college papers signed, ticket and immigration papers in hand, date and time of arrival in Trinidad finalized, and airport pick up arrangements made, Maribel made the long-awaited journey. But something went wrong with the communication, and Maribel arrived at Piarco Airport in Trinidad one night earlier than was expected. So there was no one from the college to meet her. And it was past midnight!

She later told me that a customs officer kindly offered to take her to the college, and she accepted his invitation. But when she reached the college and turned to thank him, he had disappeared! Was it her guardian angel to the rescue? She thinks it surely was! Doesn't Scripture tell us that "the angel of the Lord encamps all around those who fear Him, and delivers them" (Ps. 34:7)? Think of it! A beautiful young woman with a captivating smile, all alone, late at night, traveling in a car with an unknown man who has ample opportunity to take advantage of her either on the highway or on the lonely wooded road in the Maracas valley, but she arrives safely. Whether it was a heavenly angel or one in human flesh, we think of it as divine protection.

As word got around that there was a Cuban student at CUC with a miraculous story to tell, Maribel received invitations from churches all over the island, and their donations became part of her financial support while at college. Her story even impressed some young admirers, and one of them, an immigration officer, made it possible for her mother and brother to visit her there. A dear sister from the island of St. Thomas heard about her, rallied church members, and together they provided her with the financial aid she needed until she completed her program. I could not believe my ears when I called the treasurer to enquire of her indebtedness only to be told it was paid in full. What a mighty God we serve! Indeed He holds the wealth of the world in His hands! In her last year of college, she was diagnosed with breast cancer and many of her suitors slinked away! Friends from Venezuela supported her, our God enabled her to survive, and she completed her program and proudly marched with the rest of her class on graduation day—she was publically recognized by the president as the first student from Cuba.

With graduation behind her, the big question was, "What next?" She could not return to her homeland for the government had banned her. She could not work in Trinidad with a student visa about to expire. I explored options of her attending Andrews University or Florida College of Health Science, but those were beyond my reach. Then the cancer returned, and she had to continue her treatment, which weakened her. "Oh God," I cried, "What have I done? We need Your special guidance in this matter." Every day Gordon and I and the members of St. Thomas prayed.

Then one day she called and said, "Mom (as she calls me), I have decided to go to the U.S. embassy and plead my case." I promised to stand as her guarantor. To make a long story short, Maribel went into the embassy, and after two visits got the coveted stamp in her passport—a visa to enter the United States! How fitting that on November 21, 2007, she spent her first Thanksgiving in America with her cousin Enrique in Miami! Wow! Do I hear you call it luck? No, to us that was Providence! It was a day of victory! And so we sang, "God is so good, God is so good, God is so good, He's so good to me! He answers prayers, He answers prayers, He answers prayers, He's so good to me!"

Over the years she continued to battle cancer and at times was too weak to take care of herself. She petitioned the U.S. government and was allowed to bring her mother over from Cuba. Her quest to bring her father was denied, and unfortunately he later passed away. However, both brothers, as well as the family of the younger brother, now have resident status. Maribel is now a U.S. citizen and continues to serve the Lord in Miami. Recently she was contacted by 3ABN to do translation for an upcoming program in Indiana. When I asked her, "What's next, Maribel?" She replied with her incredible sense of humor: "This is one scenario where we can say, Thank God for cancer!" Our loving heavenly Father turned a terrible situation into something good.

Fruits of Our Labor

Farmers wait for the harvest and celebrate if it was good. Scripture gives this promise, "Those who sow in tears shall reap in joy" (Ps. 126:5). That was my experience as I labored for almost a decade in the leadership of the IAD Women's Ministries Department. It was in partnership with my heavenly Friend that I saw and rejoiced over the fruits of our labors. Here are some of them.

1. Qualitative Church Growth. As women were empowered as directors, their confidence grew. They developed skills in speaking, preaching, praying, and leadership. I remember one of them writing to let me know that she had prepared and practiced her presentation and was able to deliver it flawlessly, even though she was a bit scared. Presently many of them have been appointed to other leadership roles at the church, conference, union, and division levels.

2. Quantitative Church Growth. Women engaged in evangelistic programs such as small groups outreach and evangelistic campaigns, and at the end of five years we reported over 35,000 baptisms in twelve unions. Today women continue to lead out in outreach programs.

3. Financial Aid. Several college and university students received financial assistance from the GC

Women's Ministries Department scholarship program, profits from sales of the annual devotional book. In addition, I edited a devotional in Spanish that contained 104 devotionals to begin and end the Sabbath. Two printings netted over $20,000.

4. Women in Leadership Summit. This division-wide initiative was planned for the purpose of continuing education, recognition, and fellowship. The theme of that historic event, which was attended by 164 women, was "Female Leaders Helping to Shape the Future." At the convention they gave reports, shared experiences, and listened to seminars on various topics, including the current issues of harassment in the workplace and the glass ceiling. As you can imagine, the latter evoked much discussion. For some the glass ceiling was broken, and for others it was still securely in place. In the end it depended on the person and the place. The apostle Paul endorses that for the Christian there is neither "male nor female; for you are all one in Christ" (Gal. 3:28). The women left satisfied with a booklet of the seminars and the desire for an annual repeat.

5. Emergence of Female Authors. The domino effect continued, and female Spanish writers emerged. The books they wrote that I cherish and are part of my library are titled *Aqui Estoy Senor* (Here I am Lord), *Mi hiya…Mi amiga* (My Daughter…My Friend), *10 Cosas Para la Mujer* (Ten Things for the Woman), and a beautifully written devotional by a Venezuelan female physician. Women also showed their creative ability by their preparation of a host of bookmarks with Scripture texts or gems, and I still have some of them in my Bible and other books—all reminders of their released talents.

6. Prayer Warriors. One of the annual programs was the "Women's Day of Prayer," which was celebrated on the first weekend in March. Women used this opportunity to place their requests before God and fervently ask for His intervention. Some wrote their challenges on cards and burned them at the close of the day to signify their belief that God would destroy that problem and answer their prayer. And often when He did, they rejoiced and shared their stories of answered prayer. The West Indies Union executed a 40-Days of Prayer program.

7. Nurses Training Program. One daring women's ministries leader renovated a building for the elderly, set up a nurses training program according to her government's requirements, and equipped the students to work at that facility or at government hospitals. I was taken to the building and received a picture of the graduates from the training program. I left the ministry before that project was completed

and was unable to follow its progress.

8. Skills Training Program. In Colombia women came together to sew dresses and make soft toys. They partnered with ADRA to set up a small business to sell their products and food items. The ADRA director confirmed the success of those businesses because the women were never delinquent in repayment of the small loans they had taken.

Women's ministries gave women the opportunity to showcase their God-given gifts, maximize their talents, and use them to His glory. My mantra was and still is that the work of God today needs the combined effort of women and men under the power of the Holy Spirit to carry out the gospel commission so that Jesus can come. As I look back on those ten years of service, I must express gratitude to President Leito for his valuable help and a big "thank you" to my husband for his invaluable suggestions and constant support. On January 4, 2005, during worship at the division I was among those to receive credentials as a commissioned minister. It was a fitting climax to my ten years of service. To God be the glory!

I am especially grateful to God for His protection as I traveled from place to place in country after country and stayed alone in hotels. I never felt scared, and no one ever approached me to do me harm. It is wonderful that I never got sick. God's presence encircled me. Truly "the angel of the Lord encamps all around those who fear Him" (Ps. 34:7). All I can say is, "Bless the Lord, O my soul; and all that is within me, bless His holy name! Bless the Lord, O my soul, and forget not all His benefits" (Ps. 103:1, 2).

When leaders lead, the people often follow. And as they give themselves willingly to God, they accomplish much. And so I thank You, my Father and my Friend, for all Your blessings to me and to all of the women of IAD. Many times as I look upon the past, I get emotional when I remember God's goodness to me and direction in my life. I do not have lips enough to sing and shout His praises. Like Hannah of old I could say, "My heart is full of joy in the Lord! My strength and happiness come from Him" (1 Sam. 2:1, *The Clear Word*).

Chapter 29

Ups and Downs

While I was engaged with the departments, Gordon was executing his duties as vice president. These involved traveling to various parts of the division to fulfill tasks assigned by the president and serving in house as director of human resources. Under God the morale of the unhappy office staff was changed and the workplace returned to being a happy place. One of the activities he introduced was a candlelight communion service for the office family on the Friday night at the end of a week of prayer. The tables were arranged in the shape of a cross, and the whole service impacted the staff positively.

Working With Professionals

Another one of Gordon's responsibilities was working with Adventist-Laypersons Services and Industries (ASI). His first contact with this organization was when the division president asked him to be the IAD representative to an ASI convention on the West Coast. He was amazed at the wide range of business enterprises that were owned and operated by Adventist businesspersons and the great variety of ministries that ASI members supported all over the world. Upon his return, he recommended that ASI be established in Inter-America, and he was charged with that responsibility. Immediately he set out to visit various fields, meet with professionals and businesspersons, plant chapters, and give guidance so they could work on projects to achieve the goal of "sharing Christ in the marketplace." As a result, ASI chapters were organized in

Chapter 29 Ups and Downs

most of the unions and conferences of the division. The first IAD ASI Convention was held in Kingston, Jamaica, and the opening exercise was attended by the governors general of both Jamaica and Antigua. In British territories, the governor general is the representative of the queen of England.

During this time Gordon was upgrading and reformatting the Family Life evangelistic material into a series of study guides to reach business and professional persons, and he needed to field test it. He did so in two churches in Miami. At one of them the members were unhappy with the seminar style, although they had been alerted beforehand, and failed to support the series. In another, they complained that it was divisive because it was aimed at one class of people to the exclusion of the others. However, after some dialogue, the series proceeded to its completion, and God blessed with the baptism of ten precious souls.

These two elements converged in Jamaica when the East Jamaica ASI chapter decided to host an evangelistic outreach for business and professional persons using the Family Life study guides, and Gordon was invited to conduct it. They rented a professional venue and provided a snack for the social time that preceded each seminar, which was prepared by a well-known SDA professional caterer and restaurant owner, Lyn Thompson. She lived in a very large house high up on a hill overlooking the city. Her home was our home whenever we were in Kingston. We basked in her hospitality and relished her tasty vegetarian meals as well as her Jamaican cuisine. It was at her home that we met Yolanda Innocent, a singing celebrity who had become an Adventist, who at the time was recording her CD and singing in churches. She was to play a significant role in our ministry in years to come.

Since the twenty-one eight-page study guides were created in seminar style, the sessions were very interactive. Attendees asked many questions and were satisfied with the way the presenter answered in an intelligent and non-confrontational manner. At the end of the program, ten persons were moved by the Holy Spirit to accept the biblical doctrines of Adventism and were baptized. Among whom was the nursing director of the teaching hospital of the University of the West Indies. She witnessed to her husband, who was a lawyer, and later he too was baptized. Subsequently she accepted a call to be chair of the nursing program at the church's Northern Caribbean University.

Dark Clouds!

Many years ago I read a book titled *In Every Life Some Rain Must Fall*. And in our lives it did! In fact it became a flood, almost drowning us but for the grace of God! In 2005 we attended the General Conference session in Toronto, Canada, and after giving five years of dedicated and productive service at IAD, Gordon was not re-elected as vice president. The executive secretary and the treasurer suffered the same fate. Things like that do happen at such sessions, but the problem was that the secretary was elected to be an associate secretary of the GC, the treasurer was elected to be a vice president of the IAD, and Gordon was left with no assignment. In essence he had no job!

What was an ordained senior minister to do at this stage in his life? He was not prepared or ready to retire. As time went on, he was told he could assist in the Ministerial Department and then in the Transportation Department. The thing that stabbed my heart was that, as the re-elected women's ministries director, I was sitting in the division year-end committee meeting and he was not! Instead he was in regular work clothes handing out material to the committee members, including me, his wife. Was his fate a result of jealousy, politics, or a test from God? I told him that I was willing to sell out and return to Guyana or the Caribbean, but that was not feasible, especially since all of our children were in the United States.

In the meantime, Gordon had to fulfill an appointment that was made prior to the GC session. He had been invited to the year-end committee meetings of the then African Indian Ocean Division in Abidjan to introduce Family Life evangelism to the leaders assembled there, and we both went. However, because of unrest in the city, they moved the meetings to Accra, Ghana, instead. We had also decided that at the close of the meetings we would go to Nigeria and on return to Ghana we would visit the site where they kept and traded the slaves. The meetings went quite well. I did one of the devotionals, and together we presented the new evangelistic methodology, which they accepted as something worth trying. With that mission accomplished, we were ready to leave.

The night before traveling to Nigeria, my dear husband did not sleep a wink. All night he was up praying for guidance as to whether to go to Nigeria. I couldn't understand the hesitation because that was the plan, and he had gone to great lengths to ensure that our tickets were in hand. Then while waiting for the small plane to take off, he started exhibiting strange behavior that I could not understand. We had an uneventful and pleasant stay in Nigeria. We visited the Adventist university where they asked me to preach on Sabbath to fill in for Gordon who had declined the offer. We returned to Ghana and should have spent about two days, but that did not happen. Instead right at the airport, he decided that we should return home to Florida. Fortunately we were able to change the flight without penalty and get on one of the planes that was due to leave in a few hours.

When we returned home, the strange behavior continued. I took him to our family doctor who, among other tests, ordered a MRI, but all of the results were normal. Night by night he could not sleep. His brother-in-law Clement suggested that we contact an Adventist psychologist with whom we were acquainted. The contact was made but yielded no significant results. I cried out to my siblings in Orlando, and Magnel came to stay with us while I went to work. At times my frustration revealed itself in disgust and occasionally even in harsh treatment. I didn't know what was happening to my strong husband, and I felt drained and helpless. All I could do was pray. And Jesus never fails to hear and answer our prayers.

Not long after that Esther came for vacation. When she saw her dad, she immediately told us that he was in a state of depression and needed a psychiatrist. Typical of Esther, she went into action. She got out the phone books—no Internet at that time—and started looking. Although the Christian counselor she found was about two hours drive away from where we lived, she made the appointment and we drove the miles to see him. After several unfruitful visits, he realized he could not help and referred him to the female psychiatrist in the same building. She prescribed the medication Zolof and wanted to put him in the hospital. Then someone told us of an Adventist psychologist who was about an hour from home. He was from Trinidad and knew Gordon when he was union president, and Gordon felt comfortable with him.

Chapter 29 Ups and Downs

Demons at Work!

Some people despise the idea of a devil because they are reluctant to acknowledge the existence of a God. But the devil is real, and he delights to know that so many think that he does not exist. Here is an interesting statement we need to consider: "I would rather live my life as if there is a God, and die to find out there isn't, than to live my life as if there isn't and die to find out there is" (author unknown).

> *Gordon agonized in prayer, wrestling with God, but he felt that his prayers were going nowhere, and he found no relief.*

Often on Sabbath afternoon walks and talks, Gordon would relate how at times he would "see" the devil laughing at him and telling him he was a lost soul. Gordon agonized in prayer, wrestling with God, but he felt that his prayers were going nowhere, and he found no relief. I prayed and cried and pleaded with God, but I had to remain strong to go to work, take care of the home, drive him to the doctor, and keep talking with him. It was as if the Lord had withdrawn His "hedge" from around him and allowed Satan free rein with him as He did to Job. Come to think about it, the concept of "hedge" came from the lips of the devil. That was one time Satan told the truth! It is simply intriguing to read the dialogue between God and Satan in Job 1:6–12 from *The Clear Word* paraphrase.

In heaven, representatives from various planets in God's universe would come together regularly to meet with Him. One day Satan came also and presented himself for admittance.

And God said to Satan, "On what basis do you attend this meeting?"

The Accuser answered, "I'm from Planet Earth where I have been roaming back and forth for a long time."

The Lord said, "Have you noticed my servant Job? There is no one like him—loyal, blameless and faithful in all he does. He loves me with all his heart and hates evil."

"Do you think he does this for nothing?" Satan sneered. *"You've protected him and his family* and given them everything they have. [KJV version says, *"Hast not thou made an hedge about him, and about his house…?"*]. You have blessed whatever he does…. But if You take away everything he has, he'll turn and curse You to Your face."

The Lord said, "Very well, let's test your accusation. Everything he has is in your hands, only don't lay one finger on the man himself."

The Accuser agreed and went back to Earth. (italics mine).

And you know the rest of the story.

Gordon told of being taunted by the devil or so it seemed. He was often told that he was lost and bound for hell. And somehow he came to believe the lie because he was not connecting with God through prayer as he had been able to do previously. And Bible reading became meaningless.

I did all I could to reassure him that God had called him and ordained him to be a minister and loved him. I even held up his own book titled *I Love You*, but it was all to no avail. His sisters Dolly in New York and Shirley in Trinidad called often. My family members in

Orlando also kept in contact. After Esther left to return to her work, she too called weekly. We all prayed for him. When I had to be away from home for two weeks to attend a family and women's ministries leadership summit in Washington, DC, my big brother, Hinsie, and his wife, Lady P, gladly consented to have Gordon stay with them. Before leaving on Sunday, I arranged with Manny's door-to-door transportation service to pick him up on Monday and take him to Orlando. I was deeply concerned when I was told that he did not travel that day. When I called Gordon at home, he seemed okay and he eventually traveled the next day.

He continued to see Dr. Rupert Ryan, the psychologist, and thank God, with therapy and medication he was sleeping better as the days went by. We smile as we reminisce on the number of five-inch long tuna subs we had for dinner from Subway where we stopped after leaving therapy. It was the only restaurant in the area where we could find something suitable before taking the long drive back home. In spite of the situation, it was also a time of added bonding.

The Incredible Temptation

One week he went with me to a weeklong leadership and planning council for all division officers and departmental directors held at a beautiful seaside resort in Miami. We were all very pleased with the presentations during the week. After the Friday night meeting, we both went to the room, prayed together as usual, and I turned in for the night. He told me that he wanted to take a walk, and it was a gorgeous night with a gentle breeze and beautiful moonlight that was perfect for strolling by the ocean. But I was drained physically, mentally, and emotionally, and I needed to rest. Since he was responding to the treatment and seemed to be doing lots better, I felt comfortable with him going to the seaside alone. Chills went through my spine when later he told me what transpired that night.

He later told me that the devil was by his side, and he whispered to him as he stood at the edge of the pier looking at the rolling waves, "Just allow your foot to slip into the sea to make it look like an accidental drowning, and all this will be over." Immediately the Spirit appealed, "What about your wife, your daughter and sons, your siblings, and other family members? How would they feel?" Without parleying with the devil like Eve did, he quietly returned to the room. He also told me later that this was not the only time that he was tempted to end it all!

He later told me that the devil whispered to him as he stood at the edge of the pier looking at the rolling waves, "Just allow your foot to slip into the sea and all this will be over."

The temptation that night reminded me of other temptations. The first in the beautiful Garden of Eden with the devil saying, "You will not surely die," and Eve yielding to Satan. Then there was the one in Potiphar's prestigious home with his wife's invitation to Joseph, "Come, lie with me," as she tried to seduce the young man. "How then can I do this great wickedness, and sin against God?" was his brave reply. And then the one in the desert! "Cast yourself down." Without parleying with Satan, Jesus used Scripture and said, "It is written, 'You shall not tempt the Lord your God.'" Then He drove him away saying, "Get thee behind Me, Satan." The devil can tempt but he cannot execute. It is still the individual's choice that prevails. And in life there are only two choices.

James the brother of Jesus confirms the concept when he says, "Let no one say when he is tempted, 'I am tempted by God'; for God cannot be tempted by evil, nor does He Himself tempt anyone. But each one is tempted when he is drawn away by his own desires and enticed" (James 1:13, 14). And he pronounces a blessing on all who endures temptation. "Blessed is the man who endures temptation; for when he has been approved, he will receive the crown of life which the Lord has promised to those who love Him" (James 1:12). So the songwriter admonishes,

> Yield not to temptation,
>
> For yielding is sin;
>
> Each vict'ry will help you,
>
> Some other to win;
>
> Fight valiantly onward,
>
> Evil passions subdue,
>
> Look ever to Jesus,
>
> He will carry you through.
>
> Ask the Savior to help you,
>
> Comfort, strengthen and keep you;
>
> He is willing to aid you,
>
> He will carry you through.
>
> (Horatio R. Palmer, "Yield Not to Temptation," 1868)

Chronic depression is an awful experience, and I wouldn't wish it for my worst enemy—if there was ever such a person. It pushes its patient to say like Elijah, "It is enough! ... take my life" (1 Kings 19:4). It causes its victim to feel a small fraction of what Christ felt on the cross when He cried, "My God, My God, why have You forsaken Me?" (Matt. 27:46). During that time Gordon made a couple of arrangements to conduct an evangelistic series, but each time he canceled the appointment because the devil convinced him that when he opened his mouth to speak, no words would come out! And that was terrifying!

But after many months of waiting and hoping and praying, the dark clouds started to lift, and his depression gradually came to an end. When Jose Romero at the division office offered him a brand new computer for a scheduled campaign in Grenada, he knew that God was opening a door of hope for him. And day by day his mind, which had become beclouded by negativism, started to spark again! He could see the daystar again! And together we were able to sing praises to our heavenly Father!

We held a Thanksgiving service at our home to bring down the curtains on that chapter of our lives. And we were happy to have the presence of a number of loving family members. But above all, we wanted to express our heartfelt gratitude to my Best Friend who stood beside us all the way. Even though we could not see Him, the Lord was with us feeling the pain as much as we did. And as we look back on this experience we can sing about God's constant providence with Andraé Crouch in "Through It All."

Oh yes, I had learned to depend upon His Word. During those lonely days, robbed of a husband to stand beside me, I found comfort in reading and listening to God's Word. Chapters 38 to 42 in the book of Job were among my favorites. It is in these chapters that we find God asking Job more than seventy questions that he could not answer. In the end Job had to acknowledge his ignorance as he declared,

"I have heard of You by the hearing of the ear, but now my eye *sees* You" (Job 42:5).

We now look back on this experience with nostalgia, believing that God used it to test and strengthen our faith in Him. "Beloved," says the apostle Peter, "do not think it strange concerning the fiery trials which is to try you, as though some strange thing happened to you; but rejoice to the extent that you partake of Christ's sufferings, that when His glory is revealed, you may also be glad with exceeding joy" (1 Peter 4:12, 13). Pastor Peter, did you say "rejoice"? To us, at the time it was no laughing matter! But now we praise God for that experience.

Chapter 30

A New Day Dawns!

A Silver Lining

All three of our children sing and use their talents for God. Esther leads out in the praise team at her church, singing both contemporary songs and traditional hymns. Sammy is the professional, singing mostly the classics with his trained voice. He trains young people and helps lift their sights to attend college. No wonder, in his teen years he would lie with earphones in his ears and listen to record after record of oratorios for hours. At times you would hear him laughing. We all agree that he is an excellent teacher.

John is the singing sensation. Early in his life, innocence and bright hopes for the future were his garments. As a child at home in Guyana when not trying to read phonetically, he would sing his heart out on the veranda. The neighbors called him "Johnny Mathis." Then one day I asked him to sing at Sabbath School. When he was finished singing about the joy that comes in the morning, even when darkness has engulfed us for the night, there was a resounding "Amen!" That song, which he blessed the congregation with at Carmel Sabbath School, set the wheels of his musical talent in motion.

Around the edge of the darkness of depression, God lovingly wrapped a silver lining for our family. That precious lining was Marco. I was at work in my office one morning when the phone rang and the voice at the other end said, "This is Marco. I am a friend of Esther. I am calling to let you know that Esther left this morning. I don't know what state she will be in when she arrives because she was up almost all night making adjustments to her dissertation and then packing and catching the flight home, but she should arrive in Miami at about 3:00 p.m." We had never met Marco even though we had the opportunity to travel to Switzerland and were introduced to some of Esther's friends.

Esther had studied in Switzerland. She had completed her bachelor's degree at Andrews University, managed to get some work experience in her field in Kalamazoo, and after being dissatisfied with her lot there, went on to graduate school. It was at the University of California in Los Angeles that she completed her master's degree under Professor Francois Diederich. When he was invited to the Swiss Federal Institute of Technology in Zurich, he in turn invited his doctoral students to go with him. And Esther—a star by name and nature—took the challenge, saw it as an opportunity, and moved to Switzerland. She learned German, spent about four years there, and completed her doctor of natural science degree. Her dissertation is as follows, which I leave you to interpret: "Chiral 1.1' –Binaphthyl Molecular Clefts for the Selective Recognition and Enantioselective Complexation of Excitatory Amino Acid Derivatives."

Esther and Marco

Let me pause here to tell you of Esther's journey in the field of chemistry. It started during her third or fourth year at St. Roses High School and was one of the subjects for which she signed up to take at the final external examination. We could have helped her with math but chemistry was like a foreign language to us. So she was practically on her own. I watched her spend hours literally grappling with assignments. One afternoon she came home, ate, then sat down at the piano in her school uniform, with her hair all pulled out and in disarray—a perfect picture of "I don't know what else to do to understand or solve this problem." (I just wish I could find that photograph!) At other times she would have us laughing as we sat around the dinner table and listened to her tell us about her chemistry teacher. Her hard work was rewarded with her success at the end of high school examination.

At Andrews University she slept on Aunt Lyn's carpeted basement floor in order to awaken early to study chemistry. She called her professor at all hours of the night for him to explain a puzzling section. As I write I am left with the question, "How did she do it?" She was diligent with her campus work, rising very early to attend to the cows at the farm. And she was also diligent with her studies, grappling with assignments late into the night. God has definitely rewarded her efforts. "Seest thou a man [woman] diligent in his [her] business? he [she] shall stand before kings" (Prov. 22:29, KJV).

So Esther arrived home in Miami at the expected time, and one of the first things she did was to call Switzerland. Those calls continued until one day she told us that Marco was coming for a visit. When Marco came we learned that he is Swiss born of an Italian father and American mother. He too was a scientist with a doctor of natural science degree. We were glad to meet him, but to be honest, I was uneasy because I was not certain what to prepare for meals in order to make him feel at home. He was from Europe; we were from Guyana living in the United States. And added to that we were vegetarians and did not have the variety of vegetarian foods that are now available.

We soon realized that he was flexible and could adapt to any situation. I also noticed that he was a rapid consumer at the dinner table. This caused me to wonder whether he was just

Chapter 30 A New Day Dawns!

being kind. Esther set my heart at ease when she told me that he eats fast, especially when he enjoys the food. Maybe she was correct because when everyone was finished he would take seconds. We also discovered that he was a good cook. At times he prepared the meal and was very much a part of the family at worship. We loved him for his flexibility, culinary skills, and intelligent mind.

Two Wedding Ceremonies

As the years went by, Esther completed her post-doctoral program, and after several interviews she chose to work as a research scientist at Ligand, a research pharmaceutical company in San Diego. Now she was ready to settle down with Marco. Meanwhile he was working as a research scientist in Switzerland, and they exchanged visits. It was on their return from a vacation trip in Belize that one night after dinner, as we sat around the dining table, he did it the old-fashioned way—he asked our permission to marry Esther. When we said "yes," he slipped the diamond on her left hand. With a sigh of relief, they both told us that they had successfully crossed one hurdle. They were unsure that we would be favorable since although he attended church and was planning to get baptized in the future, he had not yet done so.

He said that he had a more challenging hurdle ahead, and that was the response from his father, who did not take kindly to Esther because of the racial difference. His father was quite displeased but could not deny the love they shared. On August 25, 2001, Esther and Marco exchanged their vows with each other in Zurich, Switzerland. At that time Gordon was slowly recovering from his depression and was able to do the sermonette at the church. It was a very delightful occasion. Since most relatives and friends of Esther could not be present in Zurich to share the joy, they planned a second wedding ceremony here in the United States. Sammy was the one who planned and executed the weekend activities with great detail. So there were two wedding ceremonies for Marco and Esther.

As the years went by Esther won over the heart of Emilio, her father-in-law, with her humility, love, and kindness. She was especially caring to Sylvia, his wife, during her illness. Now he sends his daughter-in-law chocolate and other gifts, and on a couple of occasions, he spent considerable time with Esther and Marco at their home in San Diego. Love is always a winner! We all love Marco. The rest of my family met him for the first time after we moved to Orlando, and as they all told me, they liked him for the way he mingled with everyone, especially the children. His greatest admirer was my eldest sister, Cynthia. Marco loves dhalpuri and roti, and he learned to make it from Gordon's sister Dolly.

Soon after marriage Marco was baptized at Maranatha SDA Church in San Diego, and he has devoted time, money, and expertise to the church, especially in the upgrading and management of their sound system. At present they attend Thirty First Street SDA Church where again he was assigned to lead out in the same role. After making his mark at the pharmaceutical company, he is on a faith venture to set up his own company in order to find a one-time injection cure for malaria and other tropical diseases.

It is the memory of bright spots like these that will keep us in trying times. No wonder Ellen White, in her comment on Israel's victory over the Philistines at Mizpah (1 Samuel 7), exhorts us to focus on them.

Let us look to the monumental pillars, reminders of what the Lord has done to comfort us and to save us from the hand of the destroyer. Let us keep fresh in our memory all the tender mercies that God has shown us,—the tears He has wiped away, the pains He has soothed ... the wants supplied, the blessings bestowed,—thus strengthening ourselves for all that is before us ...

We cannot but look forward to new perplexities in the coming conflict, but we may look on what is past as well as on what is to come, and say, "Hitherto has the Lord helped us." (*Steps to Christ*, p. 125)

The love of Esther and Marco was indeed a silver lining beyond the darkness of depression. Someone said, "Each trial we face is God's washing away the dross so that the gold can shine through." The goldsmith who burns the gold in the fiery furnace knows that the gold is pure when he can see his image reflected on its surface. So our God is waiting for His portrait to be reproduced in each one of us. Continue to work out Your will in us, dear Lord.

> *The goldsmith who burns the gold in the fiery furnace knows that the gold is pure when he can see his image reflected on its surface. So our God is waiting for His portrait to be reproduced in each one of us.*

Bright Blue Sky!

After the darkness of the night had passed away, the morning dawned, and the sun arose in a bright blue sky! Those who travel by air know that it is the kind of sky where pilots love to fly—no turbulence, just smooth sailing under a cloudless sky from takeoff to landing. That was what we were now experiencing. Some would quote the saying "Out of evil cometh good." Others would remember the Joseph story and what he said to his brothers after the death of their father Jacob, "You meant evil against me; but God meant it for good ... to save many people alive" (Gen. 50:20). We saw it as providential, as another way of God saying to us, "This was all in My plan for you. 'For I know the thoughts that I think toward you ... thoughts of peace and not of evil, to give you a future and a hope'" (Jer. 29:11).

While praying in my office one morning before starting the day's activity, the idea came to mind to suggest to the president that we adopt the General Conference model and use a husband-wife team to lead out in family ministries. This meant that Gordon and I would work together in one ministry. Providentially on that day there was a special lunch for staff, and he came and sat next to me at the table. So I was able to make the proposal. I started out by saying, "Elder, I was thinking ..." And he, always open to suggestions, answered, "What do you have in mind?" With that invitation to share, I put forward the idea. He later agreed, and not long after, Gordon and I started working together in family ministry. I was happy and extremely grateful to our loving God! And I recalled the inspired statement of Ellen White, "God never leads His children otherwise than they would choose to be led, if they could see the end from the beginning, and discern the glory of the purpose which they are fulfilling as co-workers with Him" (*The Desire of Ages*, pp. 224, 225).

So together we met with the family life advisory, developed a strategic plan, and set about to work the plan. As the result of a division-wide survey, family life emerged as one of the five key issues that required attention. This meant that family ministries was not just a department; it had become a strategic issue to be funded by the division. This gave access to thousands of dollars each year to produce and publish resources. Gordon and I became a team, and here are some of our activities.

1. Family life evangelism resources were translated into the three main languages of the division—English, Spanish, and French—and these were published and disseminated throughout the division. The materials included the campaign manual and its PowerPoint CD, and the small group lessons with their CD. As a result many pastors in all the language groups were doing family life evangelism.

2. A division-wide Adventist family survey was conducted. In order to do this, we enlisted the services of Drs. Leon and Colwick Wilson. This was a herculean task, but under God it was accomplished. This historic document identified areas of need that were addressed in our education programs. It has provided data for research by a few Loma Linda students.

3. Family life education was designed to improve the quality of family living for both pastors and church members. We developed a syllabus of ten one and a half hour seminars: Keys to a Lasting Marriage, Communication and Conflict Resolution, Singleness, Sexuality, Family Finance, Domestic Violence, Living with a non-Christian spouse, Teenage Issues, Parenting Small Children, and Parenting Teenagers. We also developed the worksheets for leaders and participants and produced attractive CDs with a PowerPoint presentation for each seminar. After retirement we added five others, bringing the total to fifteen family seminars.

4. Leadership training was done for all family ministries, women's ministries directors, pastors, and their spouses. We visited almost all of the seventy conferences in the twelve unions and conducted a two-day workshop covering the family life education syllabus and supplying them with resources. This empowered pastors to do family life education in their churches.

5. Evaluation and accountability. The leaders were encouraged to report on their implementation and make any necessary suggestions.

Extensive Team Ministry!

I often marvel at the great distances that Gordon and I traveled together. I remember that after presenting all day at one conference in South Mexico, the young energetic Family and Youth Director Benjamin Carballo drove all night to get us to the next conference. We arrived early the next day just in time to wash and have breakfast before presenting to the waiting pastoral families. When we visited each union and conference, we were armed with CDs for each leader in their own language.

To some of these unions, we were privileged to have Ron and Karen Flowers, the GC family ministries directors, travel with us and be facilitators or presenters. They commended us for the quality of the materials and were thrilled to hear for the first time a seminar on "How to live with a Non-Adventist Spouse." They traveled with us throughout the three countries of the French Antilles Union—Martinique, Guadeloupe, and French Guiana—and we were together at Montemorelos University in Mexico where we got better acquainted as we stayed in the same house for the weekend activity. They in turn recommended our materials to the other world divisions.

And so Gordon and I slept in hotels and camps, and traveled countless miles by land and air. On one of the trips I had a scare 30,000 feet above the earth in a Mexican airline. Gordon got very sick. He told me he felt nauseated, and he started to sweat profusely and had a rapid heartbeat. I called for the attendant, but there was little she could do. She gave him some water to drink while I grabbed a magazine and began fanning him furiously with my mind on high alert. When the plane began its descent, he said he needed to go to the restroom. The plane touched down and everyone disembarked but Gordon was still there. When he emerged, thank God, he was feeling much better. He was unsure of what had happened to him. As we got our baggage and met the waiting pastors, he seemed as good as ever and was back to his normal self. I can chuckle at this incident now, but at that time it definitely was no laughing matter! We were able to present the seminars without any other interruption. Maybe it was the devil giving us a reminder that he was very much alive and well.

Yes, we traveled together but not without controversy. Whereas previously we were going our separate ways, preparing and presenting our own seminars, now we had to readjust to traveling together and presenting the same seminar together. But we stuck it out and continue to present together until now. We always remember the theme song used for those seminars, and we sing it with a feeling of nostalgia.

> There is beauty all around,
>
> When there's love at home;
>
> There is joy in every sound,
>
> When there's love at home;
>
> Peace and plenty here abide,
>
> Smiling sweet on every side,
>
> Time does softly, sweetly glide,
>
> When there's love at home.
>
> (John H. Naughton, "Love at Home," 1854)

At the close of it all I had to conclude that it is advantageous to have a couple work as a team in family ministries leadership. And I am happy to see the IAD continue to use this model at the various levels of the church. God directed and we praise Him for all that was done for families in our home division.

Our teamwork at the division lasted for about four years and ended in September 2005 when I closed another chapter of my life and stepped into the golden years of retirement with "nothing to fear for the future." Yes, under God both women's ministries and family ministries were on a firm foundation, and we were satisfied. Oh yes, it was the end of the journey at IAD, and the beginning of an unknown, untried path that God was opening up to us. Little did we know that this would be just as or even more exciting than any of those that went before!

Part Six:

Happy Family Bible Seminars International

Chapter 31

HFBSI Is Born!

In my work as chaplain of the Davis Memorial Hospital, I especially liked visiting with new mothers. The reason is obvious. The mothers were usually happy that the pregnancy was over, their babies were healthy with the visible parts intact and the invisible parts functioning properly. The other reason is that I was reminded of and often shared with them the miracle of birth. It is amazing to think that the baby was conceived with the meeting of a female egg smaller than the dot at the end of this sentence with a male sperm 1/20th in length. And as cells multiply and cluster, they form organs like the heart, lungs, and brain. Indeed, a baby is a miracle! No wonder King David exclaimed, "I will praise You, for I am fearfully and wonderfully made" (Ps. 139:14)

So what does that have to do with HFBSI, which stands for Happy Family Bible Seminars International? Well every time I think about this ministry I smile. Then I "praise God from whom all blessings flow." I am amazed at the direction God gave, the ideas He placed in our minds, the persons He put in our paths, and the experiences that came our way—all were steps in the development of HFBSI from the marriage of the concepts to the birth of a ministry. But let's take it one step at a time.

"Can't be Joined Together!"

In the village of my birth lived a lovely couple who for years dated each other but they were told they "couldn't be joined" in holy matrimony. Both were professionals, both parents were in business, one owned a drug store, the other a fabric store. Both were of the same nationality. Both were of the same religion. The major reason they were not allowed to marry was that they were not of the same caste. At a traditional wedding, the marriage officer says that if anyone can show just cause why these two should not be joined in holy wedlock, he should now declare it. And for a moment, everyone holds their breath! The issue of being "joined together" is quite relevant to the birth of Happy Family Bible Seminars.

You may recall that we had moved to Trinidad because Gordon was one of the three IAD associate ministerial secretaries and evangelists. As such he was often engaged in campaigns throughout the English-speaking countries. His evangelistic programs usually had two presentations. One was a fifteen-minute family nugget given by him or any other professional of choice—I gave a few of them when I was able to travel with him—and the other was the night's sermon.

At the usual evaluation session at the conclusion of his first campaign in Grenada, Redvers Philbert, a young pastor, challenged him to marry the two components. In a typical Grenadian parlance he said, "Pastor, you're talking two times. You should talk one time!"

"They can't be joined," Gordon immediately responded.

To which Redvers replied, "God gave you brains, pastor. You can put the two together!"

Still in Gordon's mind the answer was, "No, they can't be joined." But after prayerful consideration of this seemingly impossible task, the Holy Spirit illumined his mind and showed him how to do it. He could marry each family topic to a Bible doctrine that is compatible and still keep it Christ-centered. Thus, family life evangelism was conceived.

The full definition says, "Integrated Family Life Evangelism is a divine methodology that combines vital family issues with conceptually compatible Bible doctrines in a unified Christ-centered approach." For example, the topic "Is it Really Love? How to tell" gives the differences between love and lust, then deals with the love of Christ at Calvary. The topic "Ten things every man should know about the woman" tells about the literal woman, the wife, then the spiritual woman, the church. The series of sermons was first published by the Ministerial Association of the General Conference in 1992 in both English and Spanish.

When we worked together as family ministries directors of the IAD, the division provided funding for the publication of the revised campaign manual, the sermon CD, the set of fifteen four-page lessons for small group ministry, and the small group CD. Later on we added the twenty-four eight-page study guides for evangelistic seminars and its companion CD.

The Embryonic Stage

As we were getting ready to retire, we knew that we wanted to continue to do family ministry and create the Happy Family Bible Seminars. Our first big surprise came when, at the time of our retirement, we were told that the IAD was generously donating all the unused materials in the storeroom at the division office to us and was relinquishing their share of the ownership! To us, this was definitely providential. It was a miracle! It provided us with two things. First, it gave us the impetus to legalize the organization by registering it with the state. Second, it provided us with a startup inventory for Happy Family Bible Seminars International. We took away boxes of evangelism manuals in English and Spanish, sermon CDs in three languages, and small group lessons—resources that were worth thousands of dollars.

Chapter 31 HFBSI Is Born!

In this embryonic stage, we needed expert help to maintain steady growth and bring this baby to full term. And our loving God directed us to various individuals. First, there was Jose Romero who guided us in the purchase of laptop computers and printer and set up our website, even before we left Miami. And he did this as a donation. In Orlando we discussed the nonprofit idea with Aubrey who connected us with a colleague who was competent in that area. After consultation he helped in filing the documents and registering the ministry with the state of Florida. This occurred at just the right time because soon after he got very sick and could not function. Registration with the state made the name "Happy Family Bible Seminars International" official. Indeed, the baby was growing quickly.

Then when we needed a few persons to be members to satisfy registration requirements, we were directed to persons living in the area with whom we were well acquainted. At our first meeting they in turn recommended other individuals to form the board of directors. The registration process started on August 25, 2005, papers were filed on September 7, 2005, and the organization was incorporated on September 12, 2005. The individual elected to the post of treasurer was Roland Thomson, and he has been our treasurer ever since! Our partnership with Roland dated back to 1991 when Gordon served as president of the Caribbean Union and Roland was the treasurer.

We advertised our services, did presentations when invited, and felt very comfortable with the development. The first board meeting of six directors convened on May 16, 2007. After orientation to the ministry, the board adopted the mission and vision statements, objectives, and the constitution and bylaws. The officers were elected, and a publicist was named. Thus was born a ministry known as Happy Family Bible Seminars International. And we say, "To God be the glory!"

Growing Pains

Every newborn has growing pains. Soon after birth, some babies have to be "slapped gently" by the physician to inspire them to take their first breath of life. And isn't that similar to what the Creator did to Adam as his form of dust lay prostrate on the ground? Instead of a slap, God in essence bent down and kissed Adam as He "breathed into his nostrils the breath of life; and man became a living being" (Gen. 2:7). Other babies need to learn the art of sucking from the mother's breast in order to get the life-giving milk. Still others develop different kinds of illnesses that need extended care.

Anyone who has started a ministry will confirm that there are growing pains, and HFBSI was no different. Here was a husband and wife team starting out with no experience in setting up a ministry but with faith that this was what God wanted us to do. What were some of our growing pains?

The first one was financial. Our income was low and our expenses were high. By the second board meeting, we faced the stark reality that we needed much more income to print the upgraded study guides. The quote from Colombia, where most of our printing was done when we were at the division, was about $10,000. The thought of applying for tax-exempt status was previously discussed and shelved since we did not think we needed it. Now we knew that we did! At our third board meeting on November 12, 2007, it was decided to seek expert help. In the meantime, we used a significant portion of our retirement income to keep the ministry afloat.

As we investigated we discovered, much to our dismay, that any organization seeking tax-exempt status needed to apply within three years of its incorporation. And we were just three months away from that deadline! We definitely needed urgent professional help, and Alvin, who had helped us with the registration, was sick. We were advised to use a lawyer, but that was too expensive for our very small ministry! We were also told that the process had taken more than a year for some organizations. Then we were directed to a retired lawyer doing service for the Florida Conference. He regretted that he could not provide the substantial help needed but gave some tips and a large document with instructions.

So we prayerfully went to work. And while the prayers went up, the blessings came down! The good Lord gave wisdom and understanding as Gordon waded through the pile of material. We upgraded our bylaws and completed and sent the application just before the deadline! With bated breath we awaited the response. When it arrived we had to fulfill just a few additional requirements. And in the next official envelope, we received our 501(c)(3) certificate. This is proudly displayed in the room with all the HFBSI materials. For us, this was a big miracle! And we honor our God who "neither slumbers nor sleeps" for guiding us to success in that process.

It was C. S. Lewis who said, "Miracles are a retelling in small letters of the very same story which is written across the whole world in letters too large for some of us to see." Think of dirt on which you walk becoming a thinking human being, look at the multiplicity of stars, and there is much more. Our God is an awesome God!

More Pains!

Our second growing pain was organizational. We were careful to follow the bylaws and invited five persons to become members of the organization. These in turn elected a small board of directors, and our board meetings were cordial. However, when the board was enlarged in 2008, the sessions became stormy. Gordon and I were neophytes at this enterprise, and new board members began to point out structural defects of which we were unaware. While the information was useful and valid, the communication was derogatory and caused us a high level of concern.

So one Sunday over brunch at our home, we got together with the persons involved, had some frank discussions, and ironed out our differences. And this resulted in harmony. These discussions led to professional outcomes. One of these was the preparation of our first three-year strategic plan with measurable outcomes—a procedure that we still use today. Another benefit was the decision to host an annual conference on domestic violence to bring awareness of this monster that plagues families both outside and inside the church. Hundreds of families in several churches have benefitted from these presentations and some have expressed their deep gratitude.

Thirdly was the growing pain of visibility. Day by day we visited the offices of several prominent individuals armed with a sample of the HFBSI materials. The goal was to find a host for an evangelistic series targeting professionals and using the study guides. We visited the leaders of Florida Hospital and Florida Hospital College. We finally ended up at a church whose youthful innovative pastor was willing to participate. This church seemed ideal because it was located in the heart of an upscale neighborhood. But subsequently we became aware that the members of the church were not residents of that community and had no connection with or burden for its residents. So that project was aborted.

Then we visited with the pastor of the Forest Lake Church who was very cordial. He

Chapter 31 HFBSI Is Born! 173

tossed around ideas such as partnering with him on the pastoral team, and videotaping our program for airing on Hope Channel, but those did not materialize. Later he invited us to conduct a summer series for his church. So each Tuesday night for ten weeks, we presented a family life education seminar at Forest Lake.

Chapter 32

Miraculous Growth

Have you noticed how quickly children grow these days? It seems that in the blink of an eye the baby has become a toddler, walking and talking, growing taller and stronger. Then before you know it they are passing through those tumultuous teenage years, grappling with their identity, on their way to adulthood. It's all a miracle! It was the same with our unique ministry. Under divine direction it was growing up and moving forward.

Pastors' Workshops in North America

We printed and bulk mailed hundreds of attractive brochures with accompanying letters to administrators and pastors all over America and advertised our resources and services in *Ministry Magazine* without positive results. We later realized that our decades of ministry were in the Inter-American Division and we were unknown to the leaders in the North American Division.

But once again, God intervened by bringing us in contact with someone who could help. Pastor Samuel Campbell had recently retired and became a member of our local church. He was originally from the Inter-American Division territory but had spent many years working in the North American Division, and he knew several administrators and other leaders in the NAD. He accepted the invitation to be a member of our board, and he soon became our marketing director. He made contact with a number of them, recommended our ministry,

Chapter 32 Miraculous Growth

and then connected us with them. Suddenly new doors were opened.

Gordon was invited to several ministerial workers' meetings where he presented the concept and benefits of family life evangelism, did a sample sermon, and offered them the resources at a discounted price. The results were overwhelming! Many pastors were excited about a new method of evangelism and purchased the resources. This gave the much-needed visibility to the ministry and greatly increased the income. We were also invited to do presentations at various camp meetings in the Carolina Conference, Greater New York Conference, New Jersey Conference, Northeastern Conference, Oklahoma Conference, Ontario Conference, South Atlantic Conference, Southeastern California Conference, and Southern New England Conference.

The Dream: Happy Family on TV!

Then God gave us a dream. It was to go global by presenting the family life evangelistic series on television stations, and especially on the Hope Channel. A bold venture I daresay! So as usual, we started praying. Quite often we set aside special days for prayer and fasting. God chose to lead us through a meandering pathway to our goal. And He placed a variety of persons—some known and others unknown—to move us forward.

A few years before we had met Carlos Pardiero, president of Creation Enterprises. It was his printing facility that the General Conference Ministerial Association had used to publish the first edition of our Family Life Evangelism Manual. He was so impressed with its innovative content that he invited us to his studio and videotaped the series for his new television network called Safe TV. So we sent the DVDs from Carlos' production to the Hope Channel and requested that they air the series. However, technology had changed, and Hope TV requested that we create a new production with a live audience.

One day we received a call from my long time friend Andre Clark. He invited us to New York to conduct a week of revival at his church which was experiencing serious relational problems. Their pastor was a TV evangelist who aired the church service every Sabbath morning. The sanctuary was his studio, television cameras were present, and the service was geared toward the one hour of available air time. That was one of the issues the members had. Under God's guidance, by the end of the week a compromise was reached, and the opposing sides resolved to work with one another.

Before leaving New York we both felt impressed to explore the idea of using that church and camera crew to record our episodes. As good as that idea sounded, the pastor regretfully told us that it was not possible because the camerapersons were volunteers with regular jobs during the week. However, he directed us to a woman living in Orlando who had her own cameras and was an "expert" in filming. Since she did not have a studio, we pursued her idea of using a nearby church. And when that did not work out, we settled for a house that we converted into a makeshift recording room. Believe it or not, we still have the accoutrements from that experiment. We even transported our living room suite to the site! Since our goal was to make it interactive, we used a multiethnic group of about a dozen members to be the participants. And so with hearts throbbing with excitement, we completed the first taping at our "studio"!

After months of impatient waiting, we viewed the finished product. Our son John, who was spending some time with us, had his doubts because he recognized some flaws, but we still sent it off to Hope TV and waited, hoping that our faith would be rewarded. When we got their response, we sadly read the discouraging verdict that it was not fit for airing! The reviewer listed a host of things that were lacking, but he did not shut the door completely. There was a ray of hope. He liked the content and included suggestions to improve the quality of production. Now we were faced with the task of finding a real studio to record at an affordable price.

We heard of a studio in the Southeastern Conference. The director showed us the facility and was willing to partner with us. When that did not materialize, he introduced us to a studio in the city that was owned by an Adventist. When we met the president, Marty Jean-Louis, at his office, we were initially disappointed because he was using a converted storage facility! But when he showed us his professional studio, and we saw his camera crew, we were very impressed. We were happy that our search had come to an end.

Funding the Project

So what would it cost? The pilot was $1,800, and each half-hour episode would cost $1,100! Do the math for twenty-one episodes! Funds from our ministry were low because of reprinting of the twenty-one seminar style study guides, the fifteen set small group lessons, the upgraded manual and CDs. We had also revised and reproduced the education CDs, adding five new seminars to the original ten, and printed campaign preparation lessons and family nuggets. We also had to purchase a CD duplicating machine and shelving for the materials that took up a lot of space in our home. Our growing inventory had considerably depleted our funds.

So how were we to finance this large project? Our tax-exempt status gave us the advantage to solicit donations. Gordon designed a letter and sent them out with the pilot DVD to family and friends, and we prayerfully awaited the response. God came through for us. Tangible amounts came in from our daughter and her husband, various family members, and close friends. Our largest and still most consistent donor is Dr. Leon Wilson. Our partnership with Leon dates back to 1980 when he was the executive secretary and Gordon was president of the Guyana Conference.

As marketing director of our board, Pastor Campbell connected us with the secretary of the Oklahoma Conference who was looking for speakers for their annual camp meeting. We did presentations during the day, and Gordon spoke at their pastors' meetings where he introduced family life evangelism. The administrators of the conference were very impressed and visualized the evangelistic triumphs that this strategy would bring. We could hardly believe it when the president invited us to become consultants for the conference! We would be there to do programs for a few weeks each quarter. Besides travel and accommodation, we would receive a monthly stipend of $1,500. That was an awesome miracle!

Many of the pastors were excited! One even bought 200 sets of the eight-page study guides to conduct a program, sure of an abundant harvest of souls. Unfortunately, the highly conservative members of the older generation, uncomfortable with the topics on sexuality, forced him to abort the project. We traveled there back and forth for one year, training pastors to use the evangelism and educational material, church elders to develop and present effective sermons, and women to build relationships in the church.

We channeled all of our income from the conference into the ministry. And yes, you guessed it! With that income together with

Chapter 32 Miraculous Growth

the donations, we had enough funds to do the video recording at My Christian Films in Orlando. This reminds us of the words of Christian author Ellen G. White.

> Worry is blind, and cannot discern the future; but Jesus sees the end from the beginning.... Our heavenly Father has a thousand ways to provide for us, of which we know nothing. Those who accept the one principle of making the service and honor of God supreme will find perplexities vanish, and a plain path before their feet. (*The Desire of Ages*, p. 330)

Our heavenly Father has a thousand ways to provide for us, of which we know nothing. Those who accept the one principle of making the service and honor of God supreme will find perplexities vanish, and a plain path before their feet.

We invited a dozen persons of mixed ages and ethnicity to participate and started the recording. We did another pilot and sent it off. Finally, the series was accepted. It airs four different days and times on the Hope Channel. It was also accepted by Loma Linda Broadcasting Network (LLBN) and is shown multiple times per week. As we view these episodes on television, we exclaim, "What God has wrought!"

Every now and then our phone rings and the caller begins by saying, "I have just looked at your program." Sometimes they want to access the whole series, which is available on DVDs, sometimes they have family issues and ask advice, and other times they just want to talk. While vacationing in San Diego, we met a woman who lives in Loma Linda and was visiting the same church we attended. She instantly ran up to us, expressed her appreciation for the programs she had viewed and shared a serious family problem. We were glad to pray with her. Only eternity will reveal the number of lives that have been blessed by our television ministry.

Chapter 33

Success Stories

As for Happy Family Bible Seminars, it has become true to its name, an international ministry. It continues to service pastors, evangelists, and laypersons in North America, Inter America, South America, Europe, Asia, and Australia. Here are a few examples.

Venton Charles, a lay preacher on the island of St. Lucia, got a copy of the Happy Family manual and fell in love with it. Without attending any workshop, he preached the evangelistic sermons in his campaign and was blessed with the baptism of seventy-seven souls! A few months later he moved to another site, conducted a second campaign, and baptized fifty-two converts!

Eric R. Garloff, president of Sapphire Throne Media Inc., requested and received our permission to create his own version of the Happy Family evangelistic series. He videotaped fifteen episodes and devised an innovative plan. He contacted various pastors and offered to customize it for their churches. He did this by videotaping an introduction to each episode that included a personal greeting from the pastor with information about his church and an invitation to attend its services. Members visited in the community and distributed the first CD, then invited interested persons to visit the church's website to access the other episodes. The first two churches reported reaching 1,050 families in their communities.

Chapter 33 Success Stories

The Philippines

The Southern Asia-Pacific Division (SSD) includes countries like Bangladesh, Indonesia, Malaysia, Myanmar, Singapore, and the Philippines, where it is headquartered. Division President Alberto C. Gulfan Jr. is not only an administrator, but he is also an evangelist! And the strategy he uses is family life evangelism. In a huge campaign held in Zamboanga City, South Philippines, which was broadcast throughout the region, he reported that about 2,000 people were baptized in different places. In the host site area, there were 457 baptisms, with 111 in Myanmar and 87 people in Bangladesh.

He said, "As for me, one of the most memorable and significant results of this ministry, using your materials, is a church which has grown from 36 when we started it, to almost 150 members after a three week series in one of the cities in Guam. They continue to call their church the Happy Family SDA Church. They still meet in a tent, but have already purchased land and are raising money to build the sanctuary."

China, Korea, and Vietnam

Dr. Sally Phoon, family ministries director of the Northern Asia-Pacific Division, which includes mainland China, Hong Kong, Japan, and Korea, requested and was given permission to translate and publish the set of fifteen small group lessons for use in China. When she reported that some churches wanted to post these lessons on their websites, she was granted permission for that initiative.

Recently she wrote, " I'm so glad to hear of the 10th anniversary of Happy Family. The lessons were translated several years ago into Chinese and serving well all over China. We have distributed them far and wide and they are being used for cell group meetings and church presentations as well as for evangelism. My husband, [Dr.] Chek Yat and I have used them for evangelism throughout the last ten years in Taiwan, Korea, China, and Mongolia. Everywhere we have done this couples report positive outcomes in their relationships and ask for more outreach using this method."

And in Vietnam, church leaders also fell in love with the family life strategy. They had seen our earlier book titled *I Love You*, which is a reader's version of the Happy Family series. This volume had been printed by the Philippine Publishing House, and the Vietnamese requested and were given permission to print their version of the book. This colorful condensed volume is now being used by their colporteurs and is being read by countless persons in Vietnam. We'll only know how many have been blessed by reading it when we meet them in God's coming kingdom.

In His gospel commission, Christ says, "Go therefore and make disciples of all nations ... teaching them to observe all things that I have commanded you" (Matt. 28:19). And Jesus said that "this gospel of the kingdom will be preached in all the world as a witness to all nations, and then the end will come" (Matt. 24:14). We are thankful that God has given us the opportunity to be part of this global proclamation.

Chapter 34

"Plus Ultra!" There's More Beyond!

Before the discovery of the new world, the saying in Europe was "Non Plus Ultra!" Nothing beyond! But with the rise of Charles V of Spain, the adage changed to "Plus Ultra!" There's more beyond! The aim was to inspire Spanish explorers to venture into the unknown. And it worked! It resulted in Spanish conquests in the Americas. While we look back with gratitude to God for the miracles of the past, we are looking forward to many more miracles in the future.

Our next project is to produce a new series called Health Happy Bible Seminars. After several weeks of consultation with health professionals, the draft for the eighteen seminars was completed and field-tested. Our plan is to produce a variety of resources for this model as we did for family evangelism. This includes putting the series on television. But to do this, we had to produce a pilot episode so we can submit it to TV networks for their approval. And for this we found a studio in Texas.

Soon we were on our way to Texas to do the recording. We were pleased that everything was in place—recording equipment, a customized studio set, expert camera crew, and a makeup artist. We even received a short on-the-spot workshop from an expert on how to move from a seminar presentation to a talk show format! Joining us on the set was Dr. Schubert Palmer, a cardiologist from California. The pilot was completed and submitted, and we were ecstatic to learn from one of the television networks that this project matched their goals, and it was readily accepted.

One More Awesome Miracle

Our next challenge was to find funding. The entire project, including TV production, DVDs, study guides, manuals, lessons, and CDs, is estimated to cost over $80,000. So we submitted an application to an Adventist charitable organization requesting a grant of $50,000. Since that organization had a high level of health awareness, we were certain we would get approval. We figured that with their grant and the support of our family members and friends who had rallied to the family project the funding would be secured without any problems.

After months of waiting and not hearing from the organization, we called a day of prayer and fasting and sent them an e-mail. To our great disappointment, the reply was unfavorable. The amount of requests were many times more than the available funds, and they had approved other worthwhile projects that were in greater demand than ours. However, they left the door open for us to apply again next year.

But while we were disappointed, we were not discouraged because we knew from experience that when God shuts a window, He opens a door! Our concerned daughter directed us to another California foundation. Rejoice with me and marvel with me when I tell you that God stepped right in and that foundation gave a donation of $40,000! Did not Isaiah say, "Before they call, I will answer; and while they are yet speaking, I will hear" (Isa. 65:24)? Hallelujah! What an awesome God we serve! And with His continued guidance and blessing, we are certain that the rest of the funds will come in so that we can complete this project.

Tenth-Anniversary Celebration

On September 26, 2015, we will be hosting a Thanksgiving celebration. We will be praising God for all of His bountiful blessings over the past ten years of ministry. As we look back over the decade, we can truly say that this ministry was carried on the wings of faith and prayer. We cannot count the number of days we set aside to pray and fast, believing that He who told us "call upon Me in the day of trouble; I will deliver you, and you shall glorify Me" (Ps. 50:15) will keep His promise. On those days we put aside the secular stuff, ate a light meal until dinner, and every two hours presented specific needs and concerns before our God.

As we face the future, we are reminded of these words, "We have nothing to fear for the future, except as we shall forget the way the Lord has led us, and His teaching in our past history" (White, *Life Sketches of Ellen G. White*, p. 196). So the theme for our tenth anniversary celebration is "Blessings Yesterday! Thanksgiving Today! Miracles Tomorrow!"

Grateful for the blessings of the past, and anticipating the blessings of the future, we sing,

> Praise the Lord, His glories show,
>
> Saints within His courts below,
>
> Angels round His throne above,
>
> All that see and share God's love:
>
> Earth to heaven and heaven to earth,
>
> Tell His wonders, sing His worth,
>
> Age to age, and shore to shore,
>
> Praise Him, praise Him, evermore.
>
> (Henry Francis Lyte, "Praise the Lord! His Glories Show," 1834)

Chapter 35

The Love of My Life!

Anyone who says that married life loses its luster has not experienced true love. I have discovered that real love is not just romance. Of course true love does include romance because intimacy was created by a loving God who told Adam and Eve to "become one flesh" (Gen. 2:24), but when God is a part of the marriage covenant, there is more than just a physical connection between husband and wife. True intimacy is mental, emotional, and spiritual. And it illustrates the type of relationship God wants to have with us. "And this is eternal life, that they might know You the only true God, and Jesus Christ whom You have sent" (John 17:3).

True love is sharing both the joys and sorrows, facing tough times together, arguing, using your wit on each other, going out to eat sometimes, going to the mall, forgiving, and above all, drawing nearer to the Author of Love for "God is love" (1 John 4:8). Just as we dedicate time to our marriage, we need to dedicate time to Jesus. It is never boring to be in a relationship with Him—"In Your presence is fullness of joy; at Your right hand are pleasures forevermore" (Ps. 16:11).

My Valentine

Gordon is my forever valentine, and I am his. One day someone asked me, "Sister Marty, if you could live your life over again would it be the same?"

Immediately I replied, "I would marry the same person!" So who is Gordon Ornsley

Chapter 35 The Love of My Life!

Martinborough, fondly called "GO?" He's GO by name and nature! He is a loving husband and father to his three children. He is an innovator. And he loves the Lord and talks with Him each day with great intensity. Ever since childhood he knew he wanted to be of service to God. Gordon is the love of my life! Here are his expressions of love in the card he gave me on February 14, 2013.

A Valentine's Day Poem for the One I Love

When it comes to Valentines, we make the perfect pair—

There's romance, love, and laughter in the friendship that we share.

We care enough to listen, to trust and understand,

To build a life together, side by side and hand in hand…

We both know that we're lucky and we've got a good thing going,

Through ups and downs and give and take, our love just keeps on growing…

'Cause I bring out the best in you, and you the best in me—

I guess it takes the two of us to make a perfect "we."

And I also have another Valentine! So I say, "Thank You, Lord, for being my first valentine. And You didn't wait for a special day to express Your love. You said it long before I was born, and Jeremiah recorded it. 'Yes, I have loved you with an everlasting love; therefore with lovingkindness I have drawn you'" (Jer. 31:3). And so I can sing:

I've found a friend, O such a friend!

Christ loved me ere I knew Him

He drew me with the cords of love,

And thus He bound me to Him;

And round my heart still closely twine

Those ties which naught can sever,

For I am His, and Christ is mine,

Forever and forever.

(J. G. Small, "I've Found a Friend," 1863)

Golden Wedding Anniversary!

April 17, 2013, marked fifty years of marriage. As someone said, "That's a lifetime!" Was it all smooth going? Of course not! Sometimes it felt as if we were on a roller coaster! But in spite of the hurts, we never thought of divorce. Why? Because we love each other! We had made a commitment for life; we believed God had brought us together. And we continued to pray alone in our private devotion and together in daily morning and evening worship. We celebrated our fiftieth anniversary with family members and a few friends at the Holiday Inn on Sunday, April 13. The program was planned by the children and was indeed a delight that is forever fixed in our memory.

My biggest surprise was Gordon's gift of a trip to Martha's Vineyard, a pristine island off the coast of Massachusetts. We arrived there on Tuesday, April 16 to spend Wednesday, April 17, the exact day of our wedding fifty years before. It was like a "second honeymoon" and was indeed a memorable experience.

Here is a thanksgiving acrostic that we created for an USC alumni thanksgiving dinner. It identifies some of the things we did to keep our marriage together for five decades.

Thanksgiving Acrostic:
Twelve Things We're Thankful For

- **T is for TOGETHERNESS. We're Thankful for Togetherness.**
  Talking and laughing together, working in the yard together, and traveling together. Doing things together helps to keep us together. "Behold, how good and how pleasant it is for brethren to dwell together in unity!" (Ps. 133:1)

- **H is for HEALING. We're Thankful for Healing.**
  Every family experiences times of hurt! But we find ways to resolve our problems.
  We learn to give and take; to create "win-win" solutions, and to say, "I am sorry." As a result, hurts are healed! And the bond gets stronger! "Confess your trespasses to one another, and pray for one another, that you may be healed" (James 5:16).

- **A is for AFFIRMATION. We're Thankful for Affirmation.**
  Each of us is like a rosebush, made up of roses and thorns! We have negative traits and positive traits. We look for the roses, smell them, tell each other about them. "Pleasant words are like a honeycomb, sweetness to the soul and health to the bones" (Prov. 16:24).

- **N is for NURTURE. We're Thankful for Nurture.**
  We help each other to grow—mentally, professionally, and spiritually. And we help our children to grow. "But grow in the grace and knowledge of our Lord and Savior Jesus Christ" (2 Peter 3:18).

- **K is for KIDDING. We're Thankful for Kidding!**
  A sense of humor helps us cope with life's challenges. We learn to laugh at ourselves—with each other, and at each other! "A merry heart does good, like medicine, but a broken spirit dries the bones" (Prov. 17:22).

- **S is for SHARING. We're Thankful for Sharing.**
  To avoid selfishness, we share what we have with others. We share words of comfort, visits to the sick, and money when we can. "Go home to your friends, and tell them what great things the Lord has done for you" (Mark 5:19).

- **G is for GRACE. We're Grateful for Grace.**
  When we disappoint God, we ask for His forgiveness. We accept God's grace. Likewise, when we hurt each other, we ask each other for forgiveness. We give grace and we accept grace. "And be kind to one another, tenderhearted, forgiving one another, even as God in Christ forgave you" (Eph. 4:32).

- **I is for INDIVIDUALITY. We're Thankful for Individuality.**
  Within our unity, we learn to respect each other's individuality. We have differences that make us unique. We study how to have harmony despite our diversity. "I will praise You, for I

am fearfully and wonderfully made" (Ps. 139:14).

- **V is for VICISSITUDES. We're Thankful for the Vicissitudes of Life!**
  We hate problems, but they are good for us! They drive us to our knees and make us strong. "Beloved do not think it strange concerning the fiery trial which is to try you … but rejoice" (1 Peter 4:12, 13).

- **I is for INTIMACY. We're Grateful for Intimacy**
  Physical intimacy, emotional intimacy, and professional intimacy. We learn to draw closer to each other. "Awake, O north wind, and come, O south! Blow upon my garden, that its spices may flow out" (Song of Sol. 4:16).

- **N is for NEVER GIVE UP. We're Thankful for Never Giving Up!**
  In the early years of our marriage, we had rough times and the temptation was there to give up. Couples need to have a mindset of commitment. Say like David, "My heart is steadfast, O God, my heart is steadfast" (Ps. 57:7).

- **G is for GOD. We're Grateful for God!**
  Praise God from Him all these blessings flow! We should praise Him each morning—alone with God. We should thank Him each day in family worship. We should praise Him each Sabbath in the worship service. Every day should be a day of thanksgiving! Psalm 136 starts with "oh, give thanks to the Lord, for He is good! For His mercy endures forever" (verse 1). And the psalm ends with the words, "Oh, give thanks to the God of heaven! For His mercy endures forever" (verse 26).

Meeting My Other Lover!

As you read my story, do you see why I was so excited to tell you about my Friend? But there is one more thing. Living with my earthly lover Gordon was exciting, but what a thrill it will be to meet Jesus, my spiritual Lover and Friend! I cannot wait to see Him face to face. I know I will meet Him because He promised to come for me. He said, "I will come again and receive you to Myself; that where I am, there you may be also" (John 14:3). And He always keeps His promise!

More than that He is coming very soon! Paul declared, "For the Lord Himself will descend from heaven with a shout, with the voice of an archangel, and with the trumpet of God. And the dead in Christ will rise first. Then we who are alive and remain shall be caught up together with them in the clouds to meet the Lord in the air" (1 Thess. 4:16, 17). That is the day that I will meet my Lover, my Friend.

Just try to imagine the scene! At first there is a small black cloud in the eastern sky that gets bigger and brighter, and with the sound of the trumpet, countless hosts of angels blaze the sky! Then we see Jesus riding on a cloud as King of kings and Lord of lords! See the wicked running and calling to the rocks and mountains, "Fall on us and hide us from the face of Him who sits on the throne and from the wrath of the Lamb!" (Rev. 6:16). Hear the living righteous shouting, "Behold, this is our God; we have waited for Him, and He will save us" (Isa. 25:9). Now the angels go to the tombs of righteous dead crying, "Arise, you who sleep in the dust! Arise!" And look at the graves popping open one by one, no longer able to hold their victims! What a day of victory that will be!

Then we will take the seven-day space trip with the people of God as they rise higher and higher from the earth, leaving the devil and his angels behind. Think of passing by Mars, Jupiter, and Saturn, going higher and higher, not in space suits and air masks tethered to a spacecraft, but transported by our immortal bodies! Hear the welcome chorus of the angels ushering us through the portals of heaven! Then listen to the rich melodious voice of our loving Savior as, with a big smile and arms open wide, He embraces us and says, "Welcome home! Come, you blessed of My Father, inherit the kingdom prepared for you from the foundation of the world." It's heaven at last! The mere thought thrills me through and through! What a glorious day that will be!

Imagine the excitement as we meet and greet family and friends while gazing at the indescribable glories of heaven. On planet earth we may have been enthralled by the beauty of a hotel in Dubai or the hanging gardens of Babylon or the majestic pyramids of Egypt, but those all pale into insignificance when compared with our heavenly home. For "eye has not seen, nor ear heard, nor have entered into the heart of man the things which God has prepared for those who love Him" (1 Cor. 2:9). I think of it as the thrill of a new bride opening her eyes to a gorgeous home as her husband carries her over the threshold, and the joy in his heart as he hears her say, "Wow! You did this for me? Thank you for your love!"

Imagine meeting talkative Peter and compassionate John, adventurous Paul, faithful Abraham and Sarah, Isaac and Rebecca, Jacob and cross-eyed Leah and beautiful Rachel, Moses and sister Miriam, brave queen Esther, prostitute Rahab, and faithful Ruth, prophet and priest Samuel, and Mary Magdalene! The list is endless. As we mingle and greet each other, I keep moving because I want to see Jesus, the One who died for me! Imagine with me as we look into His loving face and touch the scars in His hands—what a day that will be! He will be the love of my life—forever!

Together Forever!

And when the thousand-year vacation in heaven is over, we will journey back to earth to live in the New Jerusalem. On the descent Christ calls to life the wicked dead, Satan, his hosts of evil angels, his war generals, and the countless host of unsaved people. The devil rallies his forces for the last great battle against Christ and His people in the descending city (Rev. 20)! The sky becomes a giant screen, and the movie of the ages is flashed before every eye, revealing the issues of the controversy between Christ and Satan. All those secret sins you think no one knows will also pass in open view for all to see. Finally Satan and his host confess their error. Those who refuse to bow to Jesus now will have to do so then! For "every knee shall bow to Me, and every tongue shall confess to God" (Rom. 14:11).

See the tears in the eyes of Jesus as fire falls from heaven and destroys Satan, sin, and sinners. Jesus weeps because those who rejected Him are souls for whom He died! He is "not willing that any should perish but that all should come to repentance" and live (2 Peter 3:9). But if we cling to Satan and sin, God is left with no choice but to destroy us in order to cleanse this planet from the miasma of sin.

When the fire consumes the wicked, the holy city completes its descent, and God makes all things new. It will be like Eden. And in that fair land, we will live together forever free from the curse of sin! There will be no more pain, nor death, nor sorrow, nor crying (Rev. 21). And we

Chapter 35 The Love of My Life!

will live with Jesus, not fifty years, not even seventy years or 100 years, but forever. And forever is a long, long time! Thinking of that time, Carrie Ellis Breck exclaimed,

> Face to face with Christ, my Savior,
>
> Face to face—what will it be,
>
> When with rapture I behold Him,
>
> Jesus Christ who died for me?
>
> Face to face shall I behold Him,
>
> Far beyond the starry sky;
>
> Face to face in all His glory,
>
> I shall see Him by and by!
>
> ("Face to Face," 1898)

So forever and ever, I will abide with my Best Friend and Lover. Ellen G. White puts it this way, "The great controversy is ended. Sin and sinners are no more. The entire universe is clean. One pulse of harmony and gladness beats through the vast creation. From Him who created all, flow life and light and gladness, throughout the realms of illimitable space. From the minutest atom to the greatest world, all things, animate and inanimate, in their unshadowed beauty and perfect joy, declare that God is love" (*The Great Controversy*, p. 678).

> *The Bible closes with an open invitation for all. "And the Spirit and the bride say, 'Come!' And let him who hears say, 'Come!' And let him who thirsts come."*

The Bible closes with an open invitation for all. "And the Spirit and the bride say, 'Come!' And let him who hears say, 'Come!' And let him who thirsts come." (Rev. 22:17). So as I close my story, I invite you, my dear ones, to "come and go with me to My Father's house. There'll be joy, joy, joy!"

The story is told of a mother who, knowing that her time of departure was at hand, called her children to her bedside. As she warmly embraced the first child with loving heart and halting breath she said, "Goodnight! I love you. See you in the morning!" She said the same words to the second child, and to the third, and to the fourth child. But when she came to her last child, she held him very close, and whispered, "Goodbye! I love you dearly. Goodbye!"

The child was stunned at her remark and stayed back to ask, "Why did you say to the others, 'goodnight' but to me you said 'goodbye?'" With labored breath, she said, "My child, your siblings all know, love, and serve Jesus and will be saved. So I will see them on resurrection morning. But since you have not committed your life to Christ, I may not see you again. So with aching heart I have to say 'goodbye!' But remember, you still have time to make the right choice!" And then she closed her eyes and went to sleep to await the call of the Life-giver.

So what will it be for you? My prayer is that for all of you, my children, it will be "Goodnight!" And that is also my wish for you, dear reader, "Goodnight! See you in the morning!"

Bibliography

Hymnary.org. All of the hymns listed in the book are in the public domain. The hymn lyrics and publication date for each hymn were verified using this website.

White, Ellen G. *Christ's Object Lessons.* Washington, DC: Review and Herald Publishing Association, 1900.

———. *The Desire of Age.* Mountain View, CA: Pacific Press Publishing Association, 1898.

———. *Education.* Mountain View, CA: Pacific Press Publishing Association, 1903.

———. *The Great Controversy.* Mountain View, CA: Pacific Press Publishing Association, 1911.

———. *Life Sketches of Ellen G. White.* Mountain View, CA: Pacific Press Publishing Association, 1915.

———. *Patriarchs and Prophets.* Washington, DC: Review and Herald Publishing Association, 1890.

———. *Steps to Christ.* Mountain View, CA: Pacific Press Publishing Association, 1892.

———. *Welfare Ministry.* Washington, DC: Review and Herald Publishing Association, 1952.

We invite you to view the complete
selection of titles we publish at:

www.TEACHServices.com

Scan with your mobile
device to go directly
to our website.

Please write or email us your praises, reactions, or
thoughts about this or any other book we publish at:

P.O. Box 954
Ringgold, GA 30736

info@TEACHServices.com

TEACH Services, Inc., titles may be purchased in bulk for
educational, business, fund-raising, or sales promotional use.
For information, please e-mail:

BulkSales@TEACHServices.com

Finally, if you are interested in seeing
your own book in print, please contact us at

publishing@TEACHServices.com

We would be happy to review your manuscript for free.

www.ingramcontent.com/pod-product-compliance
Lightning Source LLC
Chambersburg PA
CBHW081837170426
43199CB00017B/2759